I once spoke in tongues

I once spoke in tongues

by Wayne A. Robinson

FORUM HOUSE/Publishers
Atlanta

Printed in the United States of America

Library of Congress catalog card number: 73-75315
ISBN: 0-913618-10-1

A list of reference sources for which we give grateful acknowledg-
ment can be found at the end of this book.

To Sharon

PREFACE: A DIFFERENT PERSPECTIVE

Many books on speaking in tongues have been published. They tend to fall into either of two categories, each mutually exclusive of the other. One group treats tongues as the most important experience a Christian can possibly have, while the books in the other group are wholly critical and fail to see any benefits whatsoever. Within the last decade, there has emerged a third type, in which sociologists and psychologists have attempted to apply scientific analysis to the tongues phenomenon. Because of their professional training and interest, they reflect a relative lack of theological or denominational bias. Their conclusions have leaned toward a more favorable interpretation.

This book, though, falls in none of the above categories. While some psychological and sociological implications are considered, they do not constitute the real thrust or intent. *I Once Spoke in Tongues* differs from other books on this subject in the following ways:

First, as a magazine and newspaper editor, I learned quite early that few of us ever write objectively about any situation or subject — especially those in which we are personally involved. No matter how lofty our intent, we are too much a part of the subject to transcend totally our individual feelings and personal opinions.

Given this reality, the alternative is clear; namely, we must try to be fair, to give each side of an issue a hearing. We can recognize and acknowledge our own bias and prejudice, yet, at the same time, commit ourselves to hearing out and representing others who have different perspectives.

Perhaps my strong feelings on this have been heightened because of my close relationship with one of the most controversial religious figures of the twentieth century, Oral Roberts. My grandparents, the late Mr. and Mrs. J. P. Pryor, were instrumental in Oral's parents leaving the Methodist Church to join a Pentecostal one — the denomination of my own family. As a young man, Oral was a Pentecostal pastor and evangelist in my home state, Oklahoma. Then, in the sixties, I became associated with him in a variety of positions, including editor-in-chief of his publications, executive producer of his new television series, and vice president for public affairs in his university.

This background has permitted me to know Oral Roberts as a person, first, and then as a public figure. I know him to be scrupulously honest and moral, compassionate to a fault for people in need. During the time in which I was associated with him, Oral made decisions that created much controversy but also enhanced his national and international image. Some of these included dropping his public crusades, joining the Methodist Church, and starting a new television series with an entertainment format. Additionally, Oral Roberts University became fully accredited, and his basketball team became contenders for best in the nation.

Virtually all these developments precipitated requests for interviews from newspapers, magazines, columnists, and network television and radio reporters and commentators. In a typical month, February, 1972, newspapers alone carried 3,234 stories about some phase of the Oral Roberts concerns. While I was coordinating much of this publicity and exposure, my intent was never to secure acceptance of his beliefs. Professionally or personally, that was irrelevant. But I was concerned for the media to have *all* the information available.

Beyond this, I encouraged them to be fair. "Write what you see, hear, and know to be so – good, bad, or indifferent." That kind of treatment, whether of politicians or religious figures, is all that can be hoped for.

As I have written this book on tongues, itself a controversial topic, fairness has been a very intentional aim. *I Once Spoke in Tongues* does not purport to be an *objective* study; in fact, it draws some very subjective conclusions. But, I do try to treat fairly the different positions and diverse understandings. There are some fine, honest men and women who speak in tongues. There are many equally honest and admirable persons who don't accept the validity of the tongues experience. Each viewpoint deserves fair treatment.

Second, *I Once Spoke in Tongues* is an effort to increase understanding. Theologian Schubert Ogden has aptly said: "Before you can say 'I agree' or 'I disagree' with another position, you should be able to say, 'I understand.' " I hope that the pages which follow will contribute to an understanding of both tongues itself and of its adherents.

The third characteristic of *I Once Spoke in Tongues* is its expression of my personal beliefs. There was a time when I could have written a book advocating speaking in tongues. There was a later period of reaction when I was completely against the practice. However, in the past few years, I have become more and more convinced that *the* test, not only of tongues but of any religious experience, cannot be limited to the logic and truthfulness supporting it. There is also the essential question, *"What does it do in one's life?"* More specifically, does it turn a person inward to self-concern and selfish interests, or does it open him up to others and to their needs?

I know people who testify that speaking in tongues

has been the great liberating experience of their lives. But juxtaposed with them are a great many others for whom speaking in tongues has been an excuse to withdraw from confronting the realities of a suffering and divided world. For some, tongues has been the greatest thing ever to happen; others have seen it disrupt churches, destroy careers, and rupture personal relationships.

Finally, I need to say a word about the method of biblical interpretation employed. One of the contributions of modern biblical scholarship has been to demonstrate that the methodology employed in interpreting the Bible determines the answers that are received. Or, put another way, *how* determines *what*. More importantly, though, implied in the methodology is the deeper question of the warrants for faith itself. What you believe about the Bible, even before you read it, determines by and large the conclusions you will draw from your reading.

My problem was how to reconcile the differences in the methodology I now employ with that used during the period when I advocated tongues speaking, for that period comprises an important part of the book. Then, I subscribed to a literal, noncritical approach; now, through form criticism, the Bible has become much more understandable for me.

My final decision was based on the question: "Which methodology would be easiest for the most readers to understand, relative to the main thrust and intent of the book?" I decided quite intentionally to employ a noncritical methodology. The significant issues relative to tongues can still be raised without diverting attention to those topics which, though they are important, are not a part of this study.

Special thanks are due to many persons — teachers, friends, and co-workers. Particular appreciation is due my warm friend Ben Johnson for requesting this book and encouraging me to write it. And, of course, much of the insight into the charismatic movement itself was gained through my long-time friendship and association with Oral Roberts. Dr. John Kildahl, of New York Theological Seminary, was most helpful in lending me a copy of his manuscript *The Psychology of Tongues* previous to its publication. Historian G. Hugh Wamble's survey of glossolalia in *Tongues* was an excellent and dependable resource.

Publisher Ross Cockrell has been most understanding of the difficulties involved in getting the final manuscript prepared. Also, contributions from Ralph Bugg, the editor assigned by Forum House to *I Once Spoke in Tongues*, were invaluable.

And for service "above and beyond the call of duty," special thanks to my secretary, Genie Stone, for endless patience in typing and retyping — again and again!

Naturally, the one who has been a companion on this journey and a constant source of enlightenment and inspiration is my wife, Sharon. Her perspective, affirmation, and contribution are valued beyond an expression of appreciation such as this.

WAYNE ROBINSON
Oklahoma City, Oklahoma

CONTENTS

1
The Journey Beyond the Dining Room

When Papa laid his hand upon my shoulder and said, "Son, I want to talk to you a little bit," I knew what was coming. And I dreaded it. It was something that should have taken place years before. But it had waited 'til Papa was seventy-eight and I was grown, with a family of my own.

What was about to happen would be harder to take than any confrontation we had ever had. That he had waited until the car was packed and he and Mother were ready to leave confirmed my feeling that he had put it off just as long as he could. Those not so subtle hints that all was not well could no longer be suppressed.

I put my arm around Papa's shoulders and ushered him into the library. I closed the doors and took a chair facing his. He looked me right in the eyes. His lips moved to speak but quivered instead. Tears began to roll down his cheeks, but still no sound.

Finally, he managed, "Wayne . . . I don't know quite how to say this. And I really don't mean to be critical . . ."

Then he cleared his throat and said, "I don't know what it is, but, somehow, Son, you've changed . . . ."

He moved back in his chair and covered his mouth with a hand, as though he had said too much. After another moment of silence, he said, "I'll be all right in a minute, but right now I can't go on."

Papa didn't need to go on, and I almost hoped he wouldn't. Sharing his emotional pain was worse than any physical hurt. I knew that I was the cause of his grief. Yet, I felt relief that now, at last, we were finally bringing things out in the open. Papa was going to ask why I had not followed in his footsteps — why I was no longer a preacher of Pentecost.

For first, last, and always, Papa is a preacher — a Pentecostal preacher. Though I'm a minister, too, I'm a *former* Pentecostal preacher. Papa liked to think nothing had changed.

But that pose wouldn't work any longer. The facade that I had created and he had tried to accept could no longer be kept up. We were staring across a gap that was more than one between generations. Ours was a theological chasm.

Once we had walked hand in hand in a shared calling — preaching together, studying and learning together. Now it seemed as if we were miles apart.

Papa was not quite ready to accept this departure. Though seventy-eight, he still has a lot of fire in him. On this, his and Mother's annual trip up from Texas to visit with us in Oklahoma, he had brought along 300 pages of arduously prepared material on speaking in tongues and the work of the Holy Spirit. When invitations to preach became few and far between, he had refused to call it quits. Soon an expensive tape recorder had been purchased and taped sermons were in the mail to old friends — especially those in rest homes.

Now he had discovered another use for his recorder. He had brought with him 300 pages of transcription (300 pages *single* spaced!) for me to edit and then to find a publisher. Plus 110 pages of material comprising the opening of his "Pentecostal Commentary on Romans." Since there were other topics that he planned to write books about, would I please hurry the first two?

Needless to say, proclaiming the message of Pentecost has been and is Papa's life! For fifty years, he's preached in the open air, in brush arbors, tents, and church buildings. Papa has always been ready and rarin' to go.

Across the Southwest, in good times and bad, our family of eight kept on the move. We ranged from the Gulf of Mexico to the plains of Kansas. In twelve years, I attended fourteen schools. Sometimes I was way ahead of the rest of the class, at other places far behind. But until I reached my teens, I liked moving. There was something exciting about pulling up and moving out.

Invariably, though, the move came just as things were going well in our church. Attendance and finances would be up, the people responding, the prospects bright. But continuing success was somehow never in the cards for Papa. His gnawing dissatisfaction would grow, and soon he would "feel led of the Lord to resign."

Off we would go again, our old car chock full of well-worn possessions, members of the family wedged into vacant spaces. And since, in order to make ends meet, Papa bought and sold cattle, there would also be a cattle trailer straining to contain the rest of our goods. Brief stops would be made to buy bread and bologna, and soon we would be at a new church in a new city.

Here, again, it would be much the same story. For

certain, he would receive very little money. When he finally retired from the active pastorate at age seventy-two, he was receiving the highest salary of his entire ministry — $60 a week. It was too bad, he remarked, that he couldn't have had *that* kind of salary back when there were so many mouths to feed! One board of deacons declined to raise Papa's salary from $8 to $10 a week. In another church, there was no set salary — we were dependent on the special offering. The offering would be counted and the treasurer would post the amount on the register in front. One week, the total was $2.50. My brother, who had just turned eighteen, was waiting to see how much it would be. Boiling with resentment, he got up in the middle of the service, walked to the piano where Mother was playing, gave her the keys to the family car, and turned and walked out of the church. It took strong persuasion to get him to come back again.

More than any of the rest of us, my brother was scarred by that period. Though he's a millionaire now, the experiences of poverty still mark his attitudes toward money. Namely, no matter how much you make, keep working hard, driving tough bargains, and holding tightly to what you have — except where poor Pentecostal preachers are concerned. With them, he's still a soft touch.

Being the family of a Pentecostal preacher on the move meant that we usually lived on the other side of town, across the railroad tracks. Like most people of our circumstances, a lot of our clothes were either hand-me-downs or homemade. When Papa went to buy feed for the cow, Mother always went along to ensure that the print on the feed sack would be suitable for shirts or dresses.

More than once, we lived in converted Sunday School rooms, with a path instead of a bath. To be a teenager and bring friends home was sometimes testing.

But whatever the outside of our quarters looked like, inside there was a richness of love and understanding. And the bond that linked all of us was the church. Papa saw to that.

His booming bass voice bespoke great strength and confidence. I can still remember the sense of identity I would feel as our family quartet would stand to sing and then wait for Papa to introduce the song to the congregation with a short sermon. There was a contagiousness in his feelings of emotion and joy. We were sharing in something significant and important. It gave us a feeling of self-worth that a lack of material things could not take away.

As I grew older, I came to recognize that most of our "doing without" arose out of our dependence upon the tongues-speaking Pentecostal Church. In school, there was always someone to remind me of that affiliation. An incident which I remember most vividly took place when I was in the sixth grade. The school year had already begun when we moved into the new community.

On the first day, the teacher introduced me to the class. In doing so, she mentioned that my father was the new pastor of the Pentecostal Church. From the back of the room, a red-haired, freckled-face girl chirped, "That's the holy roller church!" By the time the class had finished laughing, my face was as red as the little girl's hair!

Holy roller or not, I was the son of a Pentecostal

preacher. To love Papa meant loving Papa the preacher. And loving Papa the preacher meant loving what he preached — the message of Pentecostalism. Each went with the other.

We kids sometimes wanted to buck the prohibitions — we all wished we could go to the movies, and my sisters wished they could wear make-up. Yet, despite our protests, deep down we felt that what we were wanting to do was wrong, and if we did these things on the sly, we always suffered feelings of wrongdoing.

One of those painful bouts of conscience arose when I was ten and ill with pneumonia. My father and mother were serving a small Pentecostal church in Tuttle, Oklahoma. Our quarters for the entire family were the three Sunday School rooms at the back of the church. Despite the fact that we lived in these rooms, come Sunday morning they were still used for Sunday School. And this meant that even though I was seriously ill, I was "in church."

Every Wednesday evening, there was a midweek prayer service. This particular evening, because I was sick, my older sister stayed with me so that Mother could play the piano for the song service. When the song service was completed, Mother came in to watch over me. Then, when Papa got through preaching, he came to see how I was doing, and Mother went out to pray at the altar.

Papa decided, however, that I had taken a turn for the worse. He went back into the sanctuary and asked some of the people who were still there to come in and pray that I would be healed.

Though I knew I was sick, I didn't know how serious my illness was. But when all the praying started and

Papa and Mamma began crying, I figured I must be in bad shape. That was quickly confirmed when someone prayed, "Let him live, Lord." Since I had already lost one brother while depending on prayers like these, I didn't consider my own death an impossibility. While I was pondering my fate, I became aware of a sin that I was committing. It really shook me. I would probably die and go to hell.

It all happened the day before I became ill. I had stopped in the store after school to spend a nickel which had come into my hands. I bought a box of Crackerjacks, and the prize was a forbidden treasure — a ring!

Even as the people about my bed prayed, I fingered the piece of worldly jewelry. I was desperate to rid myself of it. I slipped it off my finger and covertly placed it in my father's hand, which was placed on my forehead. Now, I was ready to depart.

Whatever Papa preached, we *believed*!

The recollection of that kind of confidence in my father gripped me as I sat now in the library facing him and reading the thoughts which were searing his mind. Moreover, I was upset because he had entrusted to my hands his own writings while there was another book project — for a radically different book — on my mind. A book of my own. The book which you hold in your hands.

It's hard for me to articulate the frustration that I experienced in writing this book. The fact that the preparation required three extensions of the publication deadline in a period of twelve months gives some idea of the difficulty. As a writer and editor, I had never before frozen so in the face of a deadline.

Gradually, I came to recognize what was slowing me

down. It was as though Papa were standing back of me, reading over my shoulder and shaking his head at virtually every line. So much of my manuscript rebutted the basic elements of my father's faith!

There had been an earlier confrontation with my father. I was sixteen then, a rebellious teenager struggling to discover my identity, fighting to gain my independence, and, at the same time, trying to reconcile inner conflict over the rigid social code of our church. The expression of my rebellion included poor grades in school, rough friends, and a refusal to go to church.

That time, too, Papa broke down. Finally, he said, "Wayne, I want to tell you a story and I want you to listen without interrupting."

What he related shook me to my shoes.

"Son, when you were only seven months old, the age of your brother when he died, you took seriously ill. We prayed. We called the doctor. But nothing seemed to help.

"One night in the wee hours, I relieved your mother from watching over you so she could get some sleep. We had propped you up on a pillow to make it easier for you to breathe. When you breathed out, there was a deep rattle and wheezing. Before you could breathe in, your little body turned blue, fighting for air.

"I got down on my knees beside the bed and began to pray. I reached out and took your hand, and I said, 'Lord, we've already lost one son, and unless you intercede, it looks like we're going to lose another. Lord, all I can say is, if Wayne will not serve you when he grows up, then take him, too. But, if he will serve you and give his life to you, then, heal him, Lord. Please heal him.' "

Remember, I was sixteen when he told me this. He looked me straight in the eyes, and with tears streaming down his cheeks, he said, "Wayne, I had rather the Lord had taken you to heaven when you were a baby than for you to go on living this way and wind up in hell."

I couldn't take it. I jumped up, ran outside, got in the car, and drove away. I found it hard to believe that he would say that. But he meant it! And his concern soon had its effect. One Sunday night, on my own, I went to a cousin's church. That night, I had a life-changing conversion experience.

Now, as Papa sat across from me in my library, I realized how much change had intervened across the years. He was a very old man, and I myself was a father. More so than ever before, I realized that you really can't appreciate how much your father loves you until you have children of your own. As I looked at Papa, I knew I loved him very much. I loved him for all the encouragement he had given me, the sacrifices he had made for me. Now I could appreciate his struggles with our constant lack of money and our having to do without. When the church failed to provide enough money for us to get by, Papa tried every way possible to provide additional funds. Sometimes that meant trading cows or farming. It meant selling real estate, vitamins, vacuum cleaners, or shoes. Whatever it took, he was not above trying.

I could appreciate the turmoil he must have felt when, after praying, pleading, and believing that God would heal my brother, the little fellow died just moments after the doctor was called. I knew that no one had experienced more guilt and grief than had my father. As a pastor, every time he prayed for a sick baby, the memory of his own child flashed before him.

But, all that was in the past. A minute-long interlude had seemed like an eternity. Finally, my father gained control. "Wayne, I'm not meaning to be critical," he repeated himself, "but it seems you've somehow changed.

"Ever since you went south to that school," he continued, "you've been different. Maybe I'm wrong, but I believe some teacher got hold of you and caused you to lose your faith and the calling on your life." (By "that school," my father meant the seminary I attended a few years back.)

There no longer was justification for pretending. Both of us knew things were different. Finally, as earnestly as I could, I said, "Papa, I *have* changed. And you're right, I *was* strongly influenced by one of my seminary professors. But not just him, Papa. There were teachers at the university, too, and, before that, teachers in Bible school. And before that Sunday School teachers. You and everyone else I've ever been close to have influenced me.

"Papa, I have reached the halfway mark in my life. I'm thirty-five, married, and have a family. I have to be honest before God about my life and obligations as I understand them. I appreciate you and Mother and all the other people who have helped me through the years. Ultimately, though, I'm responsible for the person that I am and the beliefs that I hold.

"But, Papa, the fact that I've changed in some respects doesn't mean I have any less appreciation for *you* and what *you* believe."

My father seemed moved by the sincerity of my declaration, and I could see that my reaffirmation of love for him and respect for his views helped him. That didn't mean we had resolved our differences, but I desperately believed that he could see that our love for each other and our trust in each other weren't dependent upon our thinking alike or even our believing alike.

Most of us try awfully hard to believe what we want to believe, and Papa was trying desperately hard to believe that our relationship was as close as it had been when I was in my late teens and early twenties. He stood, and again he put his hand on my shoulder. It was a tender gesture. "I just wanted to mention these things, Son. You know how much your mother and I love you and how much we want you to preach the gospel."

Arm in arm, we walked out to the car, where Mother was waiting. Soon, they backed out of the driveway and headed back to Texas, taking a bit of me with them. I found myself waving long after they were out of sight.

The next morning, I attempted to work on this book, but my efforts proved useless. Then I thought maybe I could work on Papa's material, instead. I got out his manuscript, "weighed" it in my hands, and felt its thickness. My father had turned out 300 pages. I was a professional writer, yet my efforts over a period of months added up to a mere thirty-five pages. Again, I recognized that there were significant reasons behind my procrastination — reasons that I would have to deal with right away. That's when this particular chapter was born.

As I skimmed through Papa's material, I was swept by nostalgia. Here and there, I spotted phrases distinctly Papa's. As a young minister, I had admired his phraseology so much that I had borrowed a lot of it outright.

When I compared the thesis of Papa's manuscript with my own, I recognized that there was, indeed, a philosophical and theological gulf between us. I could only hope that when my own book was published, Papa could accept my feeling that an "idea" gap doesn't necessitate a "love" gap. Only time will tell.

Eventually, though, each of us has to establish who we are in relation to the authority figures of our lives. Some of us resolve these conflicts early. I have begun to resolve mine quite late, but I'm glad that at last I have begun to pull down the facade which delayed my grappling with the issue of my emotional emancipation.

To work out one's life-stance is painful enough, but to *express* one's innermost feelings can be even more difficult. As I have written, rewritten, and edited these pages, I have continuously been aware that this book will trouble many people who are important to me, people whom I deeply respect. I could employ the crutch that, "There's nothing *personal* about it — it's all a matter of *intellect*," but this assertion is not true. We are not a brain walking around on two toothpicks. Our intellect is not distinct from our bodies and our emotions. One part of our being cannot be touched without our other parts being touched at the same time.

Still, although it is sometimes impossible for us to reach agreement on either intellectual or emotional matters, it is possible for us to respect, admire, and love persons in spite of our differences. But it takes effort!

It wasn't until I decided to go back and begin this book with an account of my confrontation with my father that the words and pages began to flow. At last, I was grappling with the basic question, "Why should someone with my background and my emotional attachments write a book which, for all the care that I am trying to exercise, will nevertheless disturb and offend some people who matter to me?"

Really, that kind of question put another way lies at the heart of the Christian faith; namely, what does it mean to be a Christian in today's world? What do you believe?

A little boy, when asked what faith is, replied, "That's easy! Faith is believing what you know ain't so." But God does not ask us to believe what we know ain't so. Closing your eyes and repeating three times with enthusiasm, "I believe! I believe! I believe!" does not change the realities of our lives or the realities of the world in which we live.

Our minds, as well as our bodies, are gifts of God. There is no moral virtue or religious value in clinging to concepts which are patently irrelevant — even incredible. As the song says, "This is the world which the Lord has made." Not the world as it was 2,000 years ago, or 400 years ago, or even 50 years ago. We are called to be honest in this world and in this day.

Yet, "honesty" contains its own brand of authoritarianism. The refusal to accept anything that we have not personally seen or felt can be just as destructive as ancient creeds protected against reinterpretation. The years which we are given on this earth are years that are full of change. Out of change comes conflict. Out of conflict can come progress. For *learning is a pilgrimage.*

A retired professor of the classics has described his own son's quest as an example of how the pilgrimage should be made.

When his son was very young, the professor told the lad the story of the Greek war upon the city of Troy. Knowing that words are elusive, the professor took the lad into the dining room. Together they arranged the table and chairs to suggest the giant wooden horse, and then the two of them "became" the Grecian soldiers who sequestered themselves inside the horse. When the curious Trojans pulled the horse within the walls of their city, the two make-believe warriors sprang out.

Later, the professor was elated to see the boy and some little friends out in the yard reenacting the drama of the horse. The professor added episodes. Later, he obtained abridgments of the epic poems of Homer and Vergil. When the lad was older, the boy read the una-bridged stories. Soon he was well acquainted with the period.

Following in his father's footsteps, the son studied the classics in the original Greek. At this point, he began to deal with the question of whether there had actually been a poet named Homer. He became immersed in the subtleties and nuances of that period, and became an authority on the religion and philosophy of the Greeks.

His pilgrimage started when, as a small boy, he was led by his father into the dining room where the two of them engaged in a make-believe game with the table and chairs. *But he had to leave the dining room and begin implementing that story in life situations of his own!*

That analogy, when applied to Christian faith, de-monstrates that if we are to acquire an increasing understanding of faith, we can't stay in the dining room, refusing to examine our beliefs and commitments. Leave the dining room we must, for faith is a *journey in self-understanding*.

When we are first confronted with the claims of the gospel, we do not really understand what that entails. To say, "Jesus is the Christ," is a leap of faith which requires a lifetime to understand. The "yes" to Christ is a response of our whole person; to understand that response is a lifetime task. Simple honesty and faithfulness can open one door of self-understanding after another, constantly moving us into new areas of transformation and renewal.

Put another way, the keys which can unlock faith so that it can be both Christian and contemporary are *understandability* and *appropriateness*.

By "appropriateness," I mean that the Christian faith is not a wax nose which we can twist and turn at our own whim and caprice . . . "I'll believe this, but I don't like that, so I won't believe it." No. There are some things so integral to the gospel that to discard them is virtually to discard and emasculate faith itself. The great acts of Christian faith (as proclaimed in scripture, confessed by creeds, and witnessed in history) are not optional. To eliminate them is to eliminate the witness of God in Christianity.

But, on the other hand, as John A. T. Robinson once said, neither is Christian faith "believing six impossible things before breakfast." The gifts that God has given us — our minds and experiences, our teachers and opportunities, the witness of scripture itself — these things speak to our faith. Here, as Reinhold Niebuhr has said, is where our interpretation of faith must have a tentative character. The insights of today may pale before those of tomorrow. Surely, it is not un-Christian to believe that God expects us to use his gifts to interpret that which faith calls us to believe.

The two poles of understandability and appropriateness require us, on the one hand, to interpret our faith in the context of a world 2,000 years removed from its story. On the other hand, they demand that we take seriously and handle responsibly "the faith once delivered to the saints."

Concomitant with that requisite of self-understanding is the demand made upon us to witness to our faith . . . to retell the story . . . to recount the meaning of the life, death, and resurrection of Jesus, the Christ.

I Once Spoke in Tongues is not simply one man's views on a controversial subject. It's not just another book on tongues. It's not just one more interpretation added to the pile. It is these things, yes; but, more significantly, it is the implementation of the task that each of us faces. Namely, how do we witness to our history, our faith, our neighbors, and our God in today's world?

2
A Reason for Celebration

"Hee lah moh shun dee lah moh sy yi. Ee tann a moh ee con dee lah moh, sun ty yah."

Finally, it had happened to me! I was speaking in tongues.

Some had told me that tongues was excess emotionalism, the result of hypnotic suggestion, a gibberish of the retarded. Further, that tongues was unbiblical, divisive, and destructive. And during four years of fruitless searching, I myself had begun to wonder. I had seen some cheap imitations.

But I had also heard people whom I respected and knew to be authentic human beings testify that tongues was one of the most significant religious dimensions of their lives. Their experience was what I wanted, and now I had it! Over and over, I was making sounds which I had never uttered before. I was standing, kneeling, raising my arms — anything to express the joy and emotion of that experience. There was no doubt: I was speaking in tongues.

My search for tongues had been a long and arduous struggle. As a new Christian in a Pentecostal church, I had assumed that I would be speaking in tongues in no time. Dedication, faithfulness, and expectation were the requirements. I was more than willing to comply.

But despite my willingness, nothing happened. Try as I might, I couldn't speak in tongues — not a word. I had taken German and Greek, but learning these languages was like falling off a log contrasted with my difficulty in trying to speak in tongues. Despite my very best efforts, I could no more speak in tongues than I could fly.

As I sat in Pentecostal services, I yearned to be able to do what almost everyone else was doing. Not only were older persons speaking in tongues, but also people my age and even younger. For them, tongues was like a native language. And, to add to my frustration, tongues had been responsible for my becoming a Christian — hearing some people speak in tongues had triggered my desire to make that step. During my search for tongues, I thought back on that experience many times.

My conversion experience followed a long period of refusing to go to any church. One Sunday afternoon, a cousin with whom I was very close came to visit. In the evening, he suggested that I go to church with him and I consented. Soon we were seated in the congregation of one of the larger churches of the Pentecostal denomination in which we both had been raised.

One of the practices of this church was to have a prayer service before the regular service, and when we arrived, the prayer service was in full swing. It was old hat to me, for a lot of churches followed this custom, but after a while, I began to squirm. This was not a routine prayer service.

An emotional tide began to swell. Soon those who, like my cousin and me, had been waiting for the regular service to begin, started kneeling in their pews and praying. One by one, they dropped, and when my cousin finally knelt, I was left like the Lone Ranger. It was a mighty uncomfortable feeling.

Throughout the building, men and women were speaking in tongues; some were speaking loudly and with abandon. Most seemed full of joy. Their faces. shone with tears as they released themselves from their inhibitions.

As I sat there, my guilt began to gnaw at me. My father was well known in this denomination. He had not only pastored for many years, but also had served in official capacities at both the state and national levels.

My rebellion had been a source of deep pain for him, but there seemed to be little that he could do about it. I hated being poor, Pentecostal, and a preacher's son. Although I was not aware of the psychological dynamics involved, whenever I got hold of any money, I spent it immediately, as if I had an inexhaustible supply. I refused to acknowledge publicly that I belonged to any church, but being a preacher's son was not so easily denied — there was no way to get around the fact of my birth and my father's occupation. Yet, in my late teens, my actions were loud disclaimers. In dress, hairstyle, habits, language, and friends, I denied that the church had any claim upon me.

As I sat in my cousin's church, the images of this life-style came before me, and I began to feel deeply convicted of my errant ways. As the emotional tide of the service began to ebb, however, my contriteness ebbed, too. The sounds of tongues began to recede as the prayer service started winding down.

But then, instead of starting the regular service as was the custom, the pastor changed the order. He called on people to give a testimony of "how God's been blessing you." One after another, they testified to the presence and blessing they had received from the gift of tongues.

The demonstration of tongues and the testimonies concerning tongues only added to the inner tension and turmoil I was experiencing. Finally, I could take it no longer. I stood to my feet — not to testify, but to ask for prayer. I then knelt in my pew. Soon I was surrounded by people praying for me. Eventually, I went to the altar and spent the next hour or so "praying through." When I got home that night, I discovered that a friend of the family had already called my folks to tell them what had happened. Later, when I told them "I got saved," their rejoicing started all over again.

Next day, the "ducktail" haircut was removed by the barber, my pants were hitched up, my shirt buttoned, and the process of cleaning up my language and habits was begun. As a symbol of the depth of that commitment, I junked my record collection. Because black singers seldom were heard on white radio stations then, I had indulged my own fondness for them by acquiring a large quantity of "rhythm and blues" records. But now they were an unacceptable remnant of my previous lifestyle, so out they went.

Yet, for all my willingness to break the habits of the past and all my eagerness for the future, tongues did not seem to be in the picture for me. I did take other significant steps. During an intensive period of prayer and Bible study, I decided to go to Bible school and become a preacher.

It was while attending Bible college that an interesting phenomenon of tongues occurred. In a revival at the church across the street, several students from the college received their first tongues experience. But they couldn't stop speaking in tongues — or so they implied. For several days, no matter what was asked or said, their response was in tongues. That event was interpreted by most of us to have extreme significance. To be so filled with the Spirit that you could not cease speaking in tongues was an infilling of herculean proportions!

I became deeply concerned about my not being able to speak in tongues. I had followed up my decision to enter the ministry and had applied for licensing by the Pentecostal denomination of my father. But there was an understanding with the licensing committee that full ordination could not be conferred until I had spoken in tongues. As a young preacher wanting to succeed, I found myself under tremendous pressure. In tongues-speaking churches, there was very little future for ministers who didn't themselves speak in tongues!

Every time I went to a worship service and an altar call was given, I was expected to be at the altar praying for the gift of tongues. When I began to have limited opportunities to preach, I would give an invitation for people to seek the tongues experience; then I would join them in searching. Needless to say, my preaching produced no new tongues speakers.

My intense quest periodically caused me to be wracked with doubt about the reality of tongues. But always there was someone for whom I had deep respect who would pray with me and encourage me. My desire, coupled with this encouragement, began to have its effect. *Tongues was real*, all right. My trouble didn't lie in tongues, itself. The trouble was that there was *something wrong with me*. I had to find out what was missing.

I began a three-pronged schedule of daily devotions:

morning, daytime, and evening. I roused out of bed at six a.m. Of all my efforts, this probably was the hardest, for I have never been an easy early riser. Coupled with this difficulty was another problem. Because of hay fever and sinus difficulties, I usually began having some clogging and drainage when I first got up. That meant that much of my early-morning devotional time was spent in sneezing instead of praying.

For the daytime exercise, I decided to fast, either during lunch hour or during the afternoon break on my job. Instead of going to eat or have coffee, I would sit in my car and read the Bible.

The evenings were simpler. I determined to read the Bible through from "cover to cover." The last thing I did before going to bed each night was to read ten chapters of the Bible.

All in all, it was an ambitious program. But it didn't result in my talking in tongues. I tried every available suggestion, from the simple to the other extreme. I read Acts over and over, sometimes on my knees, sometimes the whole book at one sitting.

I determined to analyze minutely each place in the Bible, and especially in Acts, where tongues is mentioned. I would capture the secret of those who had acquired tongues and duplicate it in my own life.

The biblical record seemed to go this way: When Jesus began his ministry, he came to the River Jordan to be baptized by John the Baptist. Upon hearing that it was Jesus, John said, "I indeed baptize you with water unto repentance: but he that cometh after me is mightier than I, whose shoes I am not worthy to bear: he shall baptize you with the Holy Ghost and with fire." (Matthew 3:11 KJ)

Then, according to the scriptures, there followed the ministry of Jesus, his crucifixion, his death, and resurrection. And just before ascending into heaven, he commanded those who were with him, "And behold, I send the promise of my Father upon you: but tarry ye in the city of Jerusalem, until ye be endued with power from on high." (Luke 24:49 KJ)

One hundred twenty of those who heard him did go back to Jerusalem. They gathered in an upper room and began waiting for the promise of the Father. Their wait coincided with the last ten days of the Jewish celebration of the Feast of Weeks, which covered a period of seven weeks — forty-nine days. The fiftieth day was the day of climactic celebration. This was Pentecost Day. "Pentecost" derives from the Greek word for "fifty."

As I carefully read of these events, I found little to help me in my personal search for tongues. But as I began to digest the events that followed, I felt I had something to go on. Because, on the day of the Jewish celebration of Pentecost, the 120 disciples of Jesus spoke in tongues.

So far as I could discover, the only criterion which they fulfilled was that they had been told by Jesus to "tarry," and they tarried. As a result, they were filled with heavenly power.

I was more than willing to tarry. The tarrying procedure for seeking tongues goes like this: Following the sermon, the preacher invites those who want the tongues experience to come to the altar and kneel. Then those who already have received this experience join the seekers to pray with them and offer help and advice. In a relatively short time, some of the seekers begin talking in tongues. For others, it is a much longer ordeal. In an evening service, it is not unusual for seekers to pray until after midnight, even though few of the "altar workers" may remain. And if a seeker doesn't succeed on this particular night, he is encouraged to keep trying.

I tarried many nights; I spent many hours in prayer at altars but no matter how long I prayed, I went without success. Apparently, tarrying was not to be the formula for my reception of tongues.

As I reexamined the Pentecost Day outpouring, I discovered that while the 120 were tarrying, they filled the time with "prayer and supplication." (Acts 1:14) "Prayer and supplication" is interpreted by some tongues speakers to mean the repetition of words and phrases such as "Hallelujah!" and "Glory!" But if the words are repeated too rapidly, they become blurred. On occasion this happened to me, and when it did, people around me would shout, "That's it, that's it!" But I knew that "it" – whatever it was – was not the phenomenon of tongues.

On another of my "magnifying-glass" examinations of Acts, I saw that one of the prerequisites, as laid down by Peter, for the reception of the Holy Spirit was water baptism: "Then Peter said unto them, Repent, and be baptized every one of you in the name of Jesus Christ for the remission of sins, and ye shall receive the gift of the Holy Ghost." (Acts 2:38 KJ)

I read this in accordance with the interpretation of tongues-speaking people. Namely, not only does speaking in tongues occur simultaneously with receiving the gift of the Holy Spirit, but also you have not received the gift *unless* you speak in tongues. According to that line of reasoning, the 3,000 who were baptized in water that day had to have spoken in tongues earlier.

I decided to be baptized in water. This decision was a purely personal one. For, although water baptism is one of the two most important sacraments of Christendom, in tongues-speaking churches it is performed infrequently with no great stress placed upon it.

It was necessary for me to make a special request of my pastor to arrange for water baptism. On a wintry Sunday morning, in ice cold water, he took me under in the name of the Father, the Son, and the Holy Spirit. Although my teeth were chattering ninety miles an hour, no tongues resulted.

In Acts 19:6, another method which resulted in the reception of tongues is described: "And when Paul had laid his hands upon them, the Holy Ghost came on them; and they spoke with tongues, and prophesied." The laying on of hands remains a popular method.

One night, I went to a revival service which featured a lady evangelist who had a reputation for helping hundreds to receive tongues. Following her sermon, I went forward to seek. She came over to pray for me, and she laid her hands on my head. I prayed and prayed, but nothing happened. When she saw this wasn't working, she put her hands on my throat and began to pat away while I continued to pray aloud. She claimed that the resulting sound was the beginning of tongues. Disillusioned, I left. I resolved to try something else at another time and at another place.

I almost resented going to church, for I found myself in a double bind. If, on the one hand, an invitation were made to come to the altar and seek tongues and I didn't go, I would feel guilty. But, on the other hand, if I went to the altar, the chances of my talking in tongues were nil. I could predict what was going to happen, I had been seeking tongues for so long that I knew better than the altar workers what the accepted procedures for receiving were. The only problem was, the procedures simply didn't work for me.

The only other method that I could find in Acts was in Acts 10:44-46. In the house of Cornelius, while Peter was preaching, his audience received tongues: "While Peter yet spake these words, the Holy Ghost fell on all them which heard the word. And they of the circumcision which believed were astonished, as many as came with Peter, because that on the Gentiles also was poured out the gift of the Holy Ghost. For they heard them speak with tongues, and magnify God."

It was preaching, then, which initiated the tongues experience. I was aware of this method, for in tongues-speaking churches, a man's call to preach is validated by his ability to influence others and get results. Many ministers specialized in preaching on tongues. The intent of their sermons was to suggest that a sincere Christian had no legitimate excuse for not experiencing tongues.

In the throes of my search, a leading evangelist of this type came to town. I debated going. Finally, I decided to go, for this particular evangelist was a long-time friend of the family.
particular evangelist was a long-time friend of the family.

I met with the evangelist before the service and mentioned I was preaching now and going to the same Bible college which he had attended. Then when the service started, he introduced me to the audience, which numbered several hundred persons. And although he had never heard me preach, he told them what a fine young preacher I was. He presumed, of course, that I had spoken in tongues.

He concluded his sermon and asked all those who wanted the tongues experience to come forward. Immediately, I was in a dilemma. After his glowing introduction, I was unwilling to reveal to the people present that I didn't have the tongues experience. I was especially reluctant to have *him* find out!

What little leeway I had soon vanished, for his next invitation was for those who *had* the experience to come and help the seekers. I couldn't sit back and not participate at all, so I went forward with the rest, as though I had tongues. I felt extremely anxious and guilty. Praying aloud at the altar was an accepted practice, but I found myself praying unusually loud to compensate for my guilt.

Afterwards, as I drove to my apartment, I was sure I had blown the whole show. The discipline, praying, fasting, Bible study — all had been for nought. To be a minister and yet imply falsely in public that I was a tongues speaker was unconscionable.

As I prepared for bed, I picked up the Bible to read my usual ten chapters. Try as I did, I couldn't concentrate on what I was reading. I knelt for a brief prayer, asking God's forgiveness and mercy. As I got off my knees and crawled into bed, I thought to myself, "The whole thing's useless. I'll never be able to speak in tongues."

As I lay in bed contemplating my future, I recognized that some of my aspirations were improbable. Soon I would complete four years at the church's Bible college in preparation for the ministry. The next year, I would complete my undergraduate degree in journalism. Yet, my becoming an effective minister and religious writer seemed remote — and all because I could not speak in tongues.

The next morning, I omitted my devotional. My first class at the Bible college — on Revelation — was at seven a.m. During the class, I thought, "If there was anything more of a mystery than tongues, it's Revelation." It was two hours until my next class over at the university, so I decided to get a haircut.

As I drove to the barber shop, I still felt extremely guilty over my experiences of the previous night. While the barber was cutting away, I reflected upon the evangelist's story of how one preacher had received the tongues experience. One day he was hitchhiking and a transcontinental truck stopped. The extra driver got out and let him in the middle. While riding down the highway, the preacher related, the Lord asked him, "Do you really want to speak in tongues?"

"Yes, Lord, I do."

"Then begin to praise me here before these two drivers."

He began praying out loud, "Praise the Lord," over and over. And while doing this, he began to speak in tongues. He didn't say so, but I imagine that the truck drivers let him finish his tongues exercise on the side of the road.

While in the barber's chair, I had a strange impression that the Lord wanted me to make a similar witness. That wouldn't be easy. I had been coming to this shop for over two years. There were several other customers waiting. Additionally, the back half of the shop was a beauty parlor, and it was filled with women.

Finally, I whispered, "Praise the Lord."

"Pardon?" the barber inquired.

I couldn't go through with it. I mumbled, "I'm just clearing my throat," and he kept cutting away.

In a little while, I was impressed again. This time, the urge was, "Try to make a convert of the barber." But when I asked the barber what church he went to, he told me he was a Jehovah's Witness. My evangelistic ardor cooled. I knew very little about the Witnesses, but what I did know about their zeal was enough to squelch any further efforts.

I was in deep depression, so instead of going to class, I went to my apartment. There, I decided it was then or never. I opened my Bible to Acts 2 — the first account of anyone ever receiving tongues. I got down on my knees and began reading aloud. When I came to verse 39, it seemed especially relevant:

"For the promise is unto you, and to your children, and to all that are afar off, even as many as the Lord our God shall call."

I decided that this catch-all included even me. I closed the Bible and began to pray. Frustration and lack of acceptance were weighing heavily upon me. I had even experienced nightmares in which I was the church's only "tongues-speaking evangelist" who didn't speak in tongues.

I prayed aloud and with intensity. I began to rehearse all my earlier attempts to receive the experience — the fasting, Bible reading, witnessing, searching. Finally, I repeated the words of Acts 2:39, but I changed the "you" to "me." Then, over and over, I prayed: "Fill me, Lord! Fill me, Lord!"

A feeling of joy swept over me. "Fill me, Lord," turned to "Glory, glory," and without any conscious awareness of what was happening, I found sounds of tongues pouring over my lips. I could control the flow, but the sounds were there ready to be said — sounds which I had never made before. The exhilaration and emotional release were beyond description.

Why now and not before? What had I done differently? I didn't know. What I did know was, *I had it*! And that was a great feeling. I decided to go back to the Bible college and tell my friends about it. As I drove, I periodically lifted my left arm out the window and spurted praises in tongues.

As I approached the campus, I was overwhelmed with anticipation. This was my fourth and final year. Since I was student body president, everyone knew me. They also knew that, for some reason or other, I had never spoken in tongues.

As I parked my car, I looked at my watch and realized that chapel would meet in a few minutes. As I walked past the buildings, praying aloud in tongues, my fellow students and our teachers ran out to rejoice with me. A mini-revival was under way. Prayer, praise, and tongues speaking lasted into the noon hour. It was a great experience.

That night, as I reflected on the day's events, there was a tremendous feeling of having been accepted and affirmed. I had passed the last hurdle!

One of my most respected teachers had taken me aside and said, "Wayne, the Lord has a purpose in everything he does. As I've watched you these past few years, I knew the Lord had his hand on you."

Then he placed his left hand on my shoulder and gripped my hand with his right. "Wayne, I firmly believe that the reason it took you so long to receive tongues was that the Lord has a special ministry for you. But first you had to be tested. Now you've passed the test."

I didn't know what that meant exactly, but as I lay awake into the wee hours, I began laying plans for my future. What a prospect! Nowhere on earth was there a more enthusiastic adherent of speaking in tongues.

3
Cutting the Tie that Binds

Now with most of my formal training behind me and no spiritual experiences lacking, I felt ready to fulfill my life's task. I was anxious to demonstrate that I was a full-fledged, tongues-speaking preacher — not only in theory, but also in practice.

Invitations to speak in Pentecostal churches began coming in increasing numbers. Now that I could testify to having spoken in tongues, there were no barriers. No longer did I have to sit contritely through sermons which seemed to admonish me personally to seek tongues. The roles were reversed. I became the exhorter. I had sanctified my life through prayer, fasting, Bible study, and a disciplined witness. As a reward, God had seen fit to impart a heavenly language.

Acceptance and affirmation by people important to me . . . a deep feeling of security in my religious life . . . the realization that there really was a tongues experience and I had acquired it: These were heady feelings.

Yet there were benefits which derived from the period when I had not been able to speak in tongues. Owing to my earlier feelings of incompleteness, when invitations to preach did come, I felt compelled to spend an inordinate amount of time on sermon preparation. The result was the development of a deep appreciation for the uniqueness of preaching.

I did not, however, master the art of preaching handily. I recall particularly an invitation which I received from one of the oldest Pentecostal churches west of the Mississippi. I got caught short. I ran out of material and was finished by 11:30 — half an hour early. The pastor jokingly told the congregation that he feared they might vote for me as pastor if I would promise to let them out that early every Sunday!

Determined not to let it happen again, when the next invitation for a Sunday morning service came, I was ready. I prepared an outline that not only made several points, but also underscored them and repeated them for emphasis. The biblical witness included a brief sweep from Genesis to Revelation, as well as a comment from Adam in the Garden and John on the Isle of Patmos. For interest and application, I gathered illustration after illustration. I was determined to preach till noon if it killed me — or, more likely, killed the congregation.

Much to my dismay, I was not introduced until 11:45. A sermon that I had intended to go forty-five minutes to an hour had to be blurted out in fifteen minutes. It was an exercise in futility.

And even when the length of the sermon was not the problem, there were other considerations. One Sunday, a singer and I traveled 135 miles to fill in for a pastor who was attending a convention. After the service, the deacon in charge invited us to lunch. I stupidly said, "Well, we wouldn't want to be any trouble."

"Okay," he said, walking away. "See you tonight."

My singer and I were flat busted. I determined then

that there was an art not only to preaching, but also to making a living as a preacher.

Receiving tongues didn't insure financial security. The more I preached, the more I depended on the offering for my income. There was no way of knowing how much it would be until it was handed to me on the last night.

During one two-week revival, I was flat broke by the end of the first week. I asked the pastor for an advance, and he gave me $25.

By the next Sunday morning, I was almost broke again. In order to have something to eat that evening, I stopped off at the store after the morning service and spent what money I had left on bread and bologna. While there, I saw another evangelist who had been in the service. We spoke briefly while our groceries were being checked, and as I left, he mentioned that he planned to attend the evening service, also. Late that night, when the service was over, the pastor gave me a check for $35. A total of $60 for two weeks' work. As I was preparing to leave, the evangelist with whom I had chatted that morning asked me to stop by his house for a snack on my way home, which I did. On the table were some of the largest T-bones I'd ever seen. After we had eaten, I said I'd better go. When I put my suit coat back on, I found a $20 bill in a pocket.

When I protested, the evangelist told me that he too had once held a revival for the same pastor — but only *once*. Then he added, "His kind are few and far between. Most pastors are more generous. Stay in there and you'll be taken care of."

His prediction came true. Most pastors were concerned and provided for those who preached for them. And never again did I have to worry about eating.

Soon there were invitations to the east and west coasts and Canada. Camp meetings and youth camps invited me. As sermons were repeated time and again, the transitions smoothed out, the words flowed, and the illustrations were paced for effect.

With more than enough sermons in the can, I discovered that to be an evangelist was quite easy. Why replace a sermon that *worked* with a new one which might not? In fact, I began worrying about not having enough work to do.

One of my fellow evangelists, to combat the appearance of his being lazy, let it be generally known that he stayed in his room in prayer and meditation most of the day and preferred not to be disturbed. He admitted to a friend that he had an earplug speaker for his portable television set. He never missed the soap operas, especially "As the World Turns."

Some of the hardest experiences were the long journeys. One night, while driving home from a revival in West Virginia, I crossed from Georgia into Alabama. After a couple of more hours, I began nodding and decided I'd better stop for a cup of coffee. I drove into the next town, and in searching out a restaurant, I circled considerably. I drank my coffee, got into my car, and turned onto the highway. A couple of hours later, I saw a sign, "Five Miles to Georgia State Line." I backed up and looked again.

I pulled out my map to see what could possibly have happened. The map told the sad story. For two hours, I had driven in the wrong direction — over a road I had already traveled.

With the passing of the months, I began to feel about my work as I had felt about going in the wrong direction on the road — *I had been there before*. It was not unusual for me to preach twenty-five to thirty times a month.

For a while, it had been exciting. It was thrilling to study and pray for hours before a service, then see the response. And people did respond! If I was preaching to Christians, there was something in the sermons to cause them to shout. If I was addressing people who were not Christians, there were stories and steps which would change their lives.

Without question, the churches themselves had been there before, too. Most of them tried to schedule a revival every quarter. Hopefully, it would be a time for reaching the unchurched. Many times, though, it was a pep meeting for the saints, with little relation to the outside world.

A classic example was a revival that I led in a large church in North Carolina. By a combination of plane and bus, I met the pastor at an agreed-upon terminal. At best, we would be late arriving for the first night's service.

When we arrived, the saints were shouting and singing. The commotion continued for some time, and when it subsided, it was too late to have a sermon. This after I had traveled all day — 2,000 miles!

On our way to the church, the pastor had asked what I did for relaxation in my spare time. He was hoping my answer would be hunting or fishing. When I answered that in the summer I played golf, and in the winter I sometimes bowled, he looked stern and said, "If you mention either one of those activities from the pulpit, you may as well pack and go back home. We don't believe in that kind of stuff here."

That wasn't all they didn't believe in. The next afternoon, while riding through town, we came to an intersection where school children were crossing. The policeman on duty motioned for us to stop, and we waited for the children to cross in the pedestrian lanes.

From one side came white children, and from the other black children. The cop only smiled when the white children yelled, "Get out of the lane, niggers!"

"That ought not to happen in America, should it?" I remarked.

For the second time in as many days, the pastor cautioned me. Racial discrimination was another forbidden pulpit topic.

Appropriate topics were sin, worldly ways, biblical narratives, holiness, and, of course, the reality of the work of the Holy Spirit, specifically tongues. That was easy to follow, for I had heard that kind of preaching all my life. I *knew* what to preach against and what to preach for. But, despite that *knowledge*, it became increasingly more difficult for me to avoid social issues.

At first, I was an ardent advocate of tongues. It was the answer to personal problems, social difficulties, and the ills of the church. With the same intensiveness which had characterized my seeking of the experience, I now proclaimed its benefits. These ranged all the way from the renewing of indifferent Christians to the revitalizing of faltering churches. Whatever the problem in a church — complacency, lack of growth, discouragement — a revival of tongues was needed!

Soon, though, without being conscious of it, I found myself speaking less and less about tongues. With the time I had available for study and reflection, I discovered that I was drawn, as if by a magnet, to an examination of my four years' journey in quest of tongues — a journey which had reached its climax in one brief emotional outburst. Since then, there had been very few occasions in which I had spoken in tongues at all, and then only briefly.

That reality began to cause deep questions. Was my initial zeal and ardor an expression of genuine enthusiasm or a cover for disillusionment? Had the all-absorbing quest resulted in an anticlimactic letdown once the goal had been reached? Had the overstatement which followed been a way of attempting to resolve internal dissension — was I denying my sense of disillusionment through an excessive advocacy?

Could the claims which I had made for tongues speaking be substantiated? If tongues were only presented as *one* of many spiritual blessings, or even *one* of many spiritual gifts, then no problem. But my interpretation of tongues (which was the interpretation of thousands who believed as I did) was to see tongues as an all-embracing, life-changing, crucially important experience.

To receive tongues was worth whatever sacrifice was necessary. And for what? An occasional outburst of strange sounds?

Was tongues worth the emphasis, or was overstatement part of a defense mechanism? Was the reason for portraying tongues in only the most glowing terms done to counterbalance the occasional ostracism and ridicule? Was that why many of the sermons on tongues and much of the testimony of the laymen emphasized persecution for believing in tongues? Was that why so many of the hymns that were sung were filled with references to the trials and troubles of this world?

One of the songs was, "I'm Going Through, Jesus."
The lyrics included:

      I'm going through

      Yes, I'm going through.

      I'll pay the price

      Whatever others do.

      I'll take the way

      With the Lord's despised few.

      I'm going through, Jesus.

      I'm going through.[1]

Implied throughout sermon, song, and testimony was
the conviction that sacrifice and rejection, while necessary, were only temporary; they paled into insignificance
when contrasted with the joy of being vindicated and
rewarded in heaven.

But I found myself asking, what if tongues became a
routine option within the life of the church? What if
there were no barriers raised, no stigma attached? With
the high price tag removed, would tongues be so highly
valued? Would tongues be the panacea it was described
to be?

And what about my preaching: Had tongues strength-
ened it in any way? I had discovered quickly that, for
the most part, effective preaching depended on a good
idea, adequate study, and rapport with the audience.
Tongues didn't make me a better preacher.

Or, take another activity, one-to-one evangelism. I had
witnessed in bars, talked to dropouts on the street,
attempted to convert hitchhikers, left tracts with tips
for waitresses, etc. But had the fact that I talked in
tongues ever won a single convert?

Where, then, did tongues contribute? Some of the
most effective and admired ministers of the day did not

speak in tongues. The great reformers and the saints were concerned with more weighty matters and gave little, if any, time to tongues. If it were so important, how were these men who didn't speak in tongues able to make such great contributions?

One Sunday night during the period when I was asking these kinds of questions, I got on the bus headed home following a revival in Texas. I happened to sit by a young Baptist preacher.

We talked about our work, the parallels and differences. We were having a pleasant conversation when, suddenly, I felt compelled to bring up the matter of tongues speaking. So, when the conversation lagged, I turned to him and asked, "Have you received the Holy Ghost since you believed?" I felt this was an especially appropriate question to a Baptist since the Apostle Paul had encountered some disciples of John the Baptist and asked them the same question. (Acts 19:2)

"Yes," my new friend answered.

This was not the answer I had expected. Based on our conversation up to that point, I was quite sure he was not filled with the Holy Spirit.

I said, "I'm sorry. I didn't know you spoke in tongues."

He replied, "I don't. But you asked if I had received the Holy Spirit, not if I had talked in tongues."

"Yes," I countered confidently, "but *speaking in tongues* is the evidence of having received the baptism of the Holy Spirit."

"Oh," he responded. Then, very casually, he inquired, "And where does it say that in the Bible?"

This was not the track I had intended our conversation to take. (Certainly Paul had better luck!) Im-

mediately I began quoting scriptures. First, Acts 2:1-4;
then Acts 10:44-47, and finally the rest of the verses
from my initial question and quotation to him, Acts 19:
2-6. I had memorized those verses long ago. When I had
finished my quotations, I was sure his question had been
answered.

But he persisted.

"Where," he inquired, "does it say that tongues is the
evidence of having been baptized with the Holy Spirit?"

When I hesitated, he began to cite evidence that
receiving the Holy Spirit was not dependent upon
tongues. He mentioned the other instances in Acts
where people received the Holy Spirit but did not speak
in tongues. Then he quoted I Corinthians 12:13, "For
by one Spirit are we all baptized into one body."

"I take that 'all' to mean every Christian, don't you?"
he asked.

For the life of me, I could not remember ever having
read that verse.

"That doesn't distinguish between those who speak
in tongues and those who don't, does it?" he asked
knowingly.

We were silent for a while, and then he evidently
decided to do a little proselyting on his own. He pulled
out a pocket testament and began reading from the
twelfth chapter of I Corinthians where Paul attempted
to get the Corinthians to place priorities upon the gifts
of the Holy Spirit.

"How about answering the same questions that Paul
posed to the Corinthians: 'Have all the gifts of healing?
Do all speak with tongues? Do all interpret?' "

Internally, I admitted that the implied answer to each
question was "no." To him, I lamely attempted to

differentiate between the tongues speaking in Acts and the *'gifts'* mentioned in I Corinthians.

Confidently, he smiled and moved in for the kill. "What about Peter's sermon on Pentecost Day, then?"

"What do you mean?"

"Well, when Peter finished his sermon, he gave an invitation to the multitude, and 3,000 responded. He told them to repent and be baptized and they would receive the gift of the Holy Spirit. What do *you* say they received?"

When I didn't answer, he read the entire verse to me: "Repent, and be baptized every one of you in the name of Jesus Christ for the remission of sins, and ye shall receive the gift of the Holy Ghost. For the promise is unto you and to your children, and to all that are afar off." (Acts 2:38f)

Again, he asked, "What do *you* say they received?"

This was the scripture that I had read aloud a moment before I received tongues. It was a favorite quotation of mine, a "preacher's sugarstick."

The "gift" spoken of by Peter *did* include speaking in tongues. I was *certain* it did, and I said so.

I knew what his next question would be. "If speaking in tongues is so important as evidence of having received the gift of the Holy Spirit, why didn't the Bible *say* the 3,000 received tongues? The commotion caused by the 120 who spoke in tongues that morning, which is recorded, would have been small potatoes compared to that of 3,000. But the scriptures never so much as faintly hint that even one of them talked in tongues. That's a strange omission, don't you think?"

This was one of the few times in my life when I found myself totally inarticulate. I couldn't think of a thing to reply. I had preached more than 325 times in the past twelve months, and now I had no response of any kind to a broadside attack upon the most crucial matter of my religious identity.

We lapsed into silence. As I reflected on our exchange, I felt that there must be better answers than I had given: Surely, others more experienced could have given more satisfactory responses. But winning or losing the debate was not at stake. What he had done was to discredit the scriptural basis for my own tongues experience — one of the last defenses I had.

I was glad when the bus pulled into my home city.

Soon after this, I was exposed for the first time to a group of charismatic Christians who were advocating a new understanding of the use and place of tongues. Their interpretation was that tongues could be spoken at will, any time, any place. In fact, tongues should be spoken every day instead of being held back for those rare emotional outbursts. And it could be done at the initiation of the person. God gave the heavenly language, but man must make the sounds. They based their beliefs upon a new interpretation of I Corinthians 12-14, parts of which were totally ignored by Pentecostals.

For the first time since I had begun trying to understand tongues, I started studying I Corinthians instead of Acts. It was as though I had never read it before. Despite all the nuances and the qualifications, it was easy to see that Paul was deliberately trying to *play down* the importance of tongues. In every list of the gifts of the Spirit, he put tongues last. He constantly underscored the importance of expressing love and pursuing the gift of prophecy (preaching or *forthtelling*).

I was intrigued, however, by his assertion that he

spoke in tongues more than the Corinthians did: "I thank my God I speak in tongues more than ye all." (I Cor. 14:18) The charismatics I had recently met interpreted this to mean that Paul spoke in tongues both *at will* and *often*.

I tried it and it worked. I could talk in tongues as easily as I could articulate the English language. The voluntary control was quite exciting. This was a new dimension, and it bolstered my sagging enthusiasm. But somehow, at this juncture, greater facility was not enough.

I had been sending in the required monthly reports listing the successful results of my revivals. Now these statistics seemed meaningless. Though I was busy and paid well, I decided to exercise my ministry in some other way. Temporarily, that turned out to be a position teaching freshmen English at a church junior college. At the same time, I was working on a master's in journalism at a nearby university.

But when I took the new job, I kept one last revival engagement. I decided to implement the new interpretation of tongues speaking that I had been exposed to. If I needed anything to bolster my decision to leave the Pentecostal ministry, that revival did it.

Several times during the course of each day and then for thirty minutes at night before each service, I talked in tongues. So far as I could tell, nothing was helped by it. In fact, the edge of expectation which I usually experienced before speaking was dulled.

This all-out practicing of tongues convinced me that not only was it as easy to talk in tongues as it was to speak in English – the *feeling* was the same. The satisfaction was not even on a par with that gained by everyday conversation. It was not a religious feeling nor an emotional one; it was simply air being pushed through the larynx.

My growing disenchantment peaked. I concluded that instead of tongues turning me toward people and their needs, my preoccupation with tongues speaking had turned me inward. Instead of driving me out into a world of hurt, lost, and lonely men and women, I had retreated to a closet to seek a spiritual high for myself. Instead of identifying myself with the meek and the lowly, I had set myself apart as a member of a spiritual aristocracy. I was trying to impress. In effect, I was shouting, "Look, people, I'm a Christian who speaks in tongues and I have the evidence to prove it!"

As I contemplated making a move, I thought of the very first non-tongues-speaking church I had preached in while still seeking tongues. Those were the days when the main challenge had been having *enough* to say. In this instance, the associate minister of a large Baptist church I had visited as part of a singing group invited me to come back and speak sometime. He thought that they had their youth service speakers planned for the next month or so, but they would be calling me soon.

One week later and only hours before service time, he called. Their scheduled speaker had cancelled. Would I come? It was inconvenient for me to go, but this would be my very first time to preach to Baptists. I couldn't turn it down.

As I hurried to get ready, I discovered I didn't have a clean white shirt. I tried a new sports shirt. It didn't fit, but at least it matched my suit. I put it on, grabbed my Bible and pen, and sat down at the kitchen table to develop a sermon. With all the material that's in the

Bible, it should be simple to prepare one sermon. Yet, in my desperation, I couldn't find a thing. Search. Thumb back and forth. Read. Nothing clicked.

I had heard of preachers closing the Bible and then letting it fall open. Wherever it opened, that was their text. I decided to try it. I only had a big family Bible. I closed it, rested the spine on the table, and let go.

Instead of falling open, it fell over closed! I tried again. This time it opened to the book of Daniel: Daniel in the lion's den.

I quickly read the story and tried to note a few points. Finally, I had developed my outline to the point of Daniel's being thrown into the den of lions. I didn't have time to finish my preparation; I had to get on the road.

I had gone only two blocks when the motor coughed — out of gas. I stood at the back of the car, signalling to passing motorists that I needed a push. They either ignored me, or honked, or cussed.

I reached into the car, got my big family Bible, and stepped back to the rear of the car again. With Bible in hand, I motioned the next car. He slammed on his brakes and came dangerously close to hitting me. When he got out, he asked in a loud voice what he could do to help. I told him I was a minister late to church and out of gas.

He put his arm around me and told me not to worry. I suddenly realized that my Good Samaritan was half drunk.

Drunk or not, I had no choice. He bumped up behind me and off we started. Within a block and a half, we were going fifty miles per hour. I waved frantically for him to slow down. He dropped back, but I tapped the brake slightly and he hit me again.

I swerved into a service station with tires squealing, purchased a dollar's worth of regular, and was off again.

When my first impression of the church's location proved wrong, I realized I didn't remember the address. I searched out winding curves and dead ends. I didn't have the foggiest idea where I was or where I wanted to go.

It was 8:15, and suddenly, there the church was. I ran in. They were standing for the benediction. When the leader saw me charging in, he told everyone to sit back down. "Come on up, Wayne, we're ready and waiting."

Out of breath, I mumbled something about appreciating the invitation and sorry to be late. I read my scripture text, "O, Daniel, servant of the living God, is thy God, whom thou servest continually, able to deliver thee from the lions?" (Daniel 6:20)

I then told the story of Daniel's commitment as a youth, God's blessings on him, and the subsequent test in the den of lions. The application was to be that if you stand true to your convictions, then when adversity comes, God will see you through.

Unfortunately, my outline had only been developed to the point of Daniel's being thrown to the lions. My last note was, "Can God deliver from a den of lions?"

"Can God deliver from a den of lions?" I asked aloud.

The next step that I had vaguely planned was to relate the account of Daniel's deliverance. However, as I stood before them, I realized that I didn't know the rest of the story. Very deliberately — while attempting to scan the rest of the chapter — I posed the question anew: "Can God deliver from a den of lions?"

There was awkward silence. Finally I said, "Yes, we know he can. But I'm going to have to be honest with you. I didn't get my sermon finished, and I can't remember exactly how God did deliver Daniel."

They laughed — and all at once I felt at home. Suddenly, they had become people — not Baptists. Then I related the comedy of errors which I had experienced trying to get there that night. They liked my humor better than my sermon.

As I prepared to close, I gave a testimony about the change that came in my life once I gave it to Christ. Somehow I hit the right note. They were visibly moved and quiet as mice. When the invitation was given, over half of them came forward to rededicate their lives.

I had left Daniel in the den of lions — undelivered. But I had been delivered. For my first time as a preacher, I felt a oneness with my listeners. And it was not in a tongues-speaking church.

I began contemplating ministering in that kind of church permanently. I recognized that such a change would mean a break with friends of a lifetime, as well as separation from the church of my family. Yet, I was ready to make it.

In no way had my evangelistic activity been a total loss. While preaching at a camp meeting, I became acquainted with the organist, the beautiful daughter of a Pentecostal preacher. Soon we were engaged and making wedding plans. One of our first big steps together was deciding to join the Methodist Church.

When that step became known to my acquaintances, there were various kinds of responses. I discovered that to many Pentecostals, the Methodist Church was the worst possible choice. One of my closest friends, who I was sure would understand me, was incredulous. His question was, "Wayne, why the Methodist Church? Anyone but *them*!"

But it was "them." And not long after that, I was engulfed in finding a totally new framework of self-understanding as a pastor in the Methodist Church.

Now, looking back from the vantage point of more than ten years later, I can better understand that decision — one that meant severing not only my denominational ties but also de-emphasizing for my own life the importance of tongues speaking.

Ten years have also given me time to develop appreciation for, instead of reaction to, that period. At times there have been overreactions and a desire to have little if anything to do with tongues-speaking persons. Fortunately, that's over. Even though the ties have been cut, I have been able to develop a renewed appreciation for the good that came from that formative period.

4
The Need
to Feel

"That man's filled with the Spirit!"

Whether the district superintendent's remark, which I overheard as I closed his door, was meant as a compliment or was said in ridicule, I couldn't discern immediately. Maybe most Methodist ministers would have been flattered by such a comment, but I wasn't sure I liked it. It seemed to imply that the district superintendent still thought of me as a Pentecostal. I had just been accepted for a Methodist pastorate, and I didn't want to be a *Pentecostal* in the Methodist Church, but a *Methodist* in the Methodist Church!

I had graduated from a Methodist university, and while there I had become acquainted with several students who planned to enter the Methodist ministry. My most lasting — and disconcerting — impression was their theological openness and diversity. Some were liberal, others conservative. A few were pious, others quite "worldly."

At the time, their diversity seemed untenable. My own denomination had very explicit articles of faith. There was no room for differences of interpretation; indeed, variation was grounds for dismissal. Now, though, as I prepared to find a new church home in Methodism, the very diversity that I had once been critical of seemed to be an asset. Believing or not believing different matters of faith became less important.

My concern over my district superintendent's remark, too, proved groundless. He was attempting to be affirmative. Initially, I had held him in considerable awe. I had learned that in addition to administering the largest district in the conference, he was generally described as the most powerful man in the conference, next to the bishop. But my awe gave way to genuine respect once we got to know each other. I learned that his doctorate was honorary, bestowed for outstanding service. He had a high school education and had worked his way up the ladder long before the current educational standards were set. That I did not have graduate seminary training didn't loom so large with him. Something else made him seem more human: Around people with whom he felt comfortable, he would not only sneak a smoke, but also have a chew. He was the type to judge people individually on their merits, and my having belonged to a Pentecostal church was of little consequence to him.

Soon, the district superintendent arranged for me to meet with the appropriate committees and fill out the necessary forms for entering the Methodist ministry. I had taken a job teaching, and by the end of the school term, I was appointed to a church in a growing suburb of the city in which I was living. They had a brand new brick parsonage, and I was their first full-time minister.

Being accepted as the Methodist pastor in this community was an exhilarating experience. The town's Pentecostal church was a frame structure out in the country on a dirt road. It was very small, poorly attended, and meagerly supported. But this Methodist church was right in the heart of things. It was the second largest, and its membership included some of the most influential leaders of the community. Being pastor of this church was a heady feeling. I was sure this was where I belonged.

The sect mentality of which I had been a part as a Pentecostal had tended to create within me an attitude of "us" against "them." Now suddenly, I was one of "them"! I wanted to forget forever the memories of little Pentecostal churches being padlocked by sheriffs because neighbors had complained of too much noise. Nor was I interested any longer in "upholding the standards of holiness" – dress, make-up, jewelry, motion pictures – against the world and worldly churches. I was one of them, and I was tickled to death.

I was determined to be more Methodist than lifetime Methodists. I wasn't quite sure what constituted "true Methodism," though, for I had only attended three Methodist churches in my whole life and had observed a total of six worship services. The churches were among the largest and oldest churches in the state, so they had little relation to the small parish to which I was assigned. My offhanded critique of their services, as compared with services that I was used to, was that they were quiet, formal – and boring. The hymns were lofty and unrelated to people. The organ had none of the "feel" of the piano and the guitar. There was no chance to pray, only to read lines that sounded as if they came from Shakespeare. The preacher spoke in conversational tones with no excitement or emotion, and what he said wasn't very interesting. What surprised me most was that when he gave an invitation, quite a few went forward.

But instead of praying, they just shook hands. When the invitational hymn was finished, he read their names and gave the churches from which they had transferred. Then we stood for the benediction.

That seemed easy enough. As I contemplated my future as a Methodist pastor, I was quite confident I could do as well, if not better.

We moved into the parsonage on Thursday. I went into town the next day and bought a Revised Standard Version of the Bible — Methodists surely wouldn't use the King James! The rest of that day and the next day I spent studying the order of worship. I had one old church bulletin and a Cokesbury hymnal with an abbreviated order in the front. I marked the appropriate spots for the singing of the "Gloria Patri" and the "Doxology." Then I memorized the Apostles' Creed and repeated it aloud several times. And that curse of the small-church minister — the mimeograph machine — I cranked it up, too.

When Sunday morning came, I was ready — an instant Methodist minister. To my knowledge, no one in my new church knew I was a former Pentecostal. They would have to find out on their own!

Since their previous pastor had been out of commission for over three months following an auto accident, the people seemed glad just to have a warm body in the pulpit. The service went without a hitch, although I felt uneasy over when to stand and when to be seated. The regular pianist was absent and Sharon filled in. The people seemed to appreciate a pastor's wife who could play the piano. Someone mentioned that she "played like a Baptist." I made a mental note. We would have to work on that!

For some reason which I did not understand, the first four Sundays attendance went down instead of up. On the fourth Sunday, it was less than half what it had been the very first Sunday. Just as strangely, the next Sunday we had the largest crowd any one could remember, with standing room only. This trend continued, resulting in the building of a new sanctuary nine months later.

On the day of the overflow crowd, a catastrophe happened. It was totally unexpected.

Following my sermon, I invited anyone who wanted to join the church to come forward during the closing hymn. On the previous Sundays when I did this, nobody had come. On this Sunday, someone did come — a lady — and this excited me. But my elation ebbed when I noticed that she was crying. I had never seen anyone cry in a Methodist service before, although in Pentecostal services it happened all the time. My old fears about being a Pentecostal in the Methodist Church surfaced. What had I done wrong? Even more dismaying, when I started talking to her about church membership, she told me she already was a member. In fact, she had been a member since infancy. For this, my instant Methodist preacher course had not prepared me.

Back when I was a Pentecostal evangelist, my *aim* was to get people to the altar; if they were weeping, so much the better — that simply meant they were under conviction and the Holy Spirit was at work. In fact, in the Pentecostal churches men and women cried openly and freely. There was an altar at which they could "pray through" with the pastor and others in the church joining with them. But my new church didn't even have an altar, only a communion table. And there certainly was no lay person available to assist her in "praying through."

After trying so hard to be a cool and confident Methodist, I found myself with a tearful young lady at the altar. When the hymn was over, I quietly asked what she wanted. Her whispered reply was that she just felt like she needed to come forward. In other words, she needed some way to express her feelings. This contingency hadn't happened in any of the three churches I had visited.

As I was to learn later, it's about as hard to be ejected from the Methodist Church over liturgical or theological matters as it is to get milk from a bull. But with only a month's experience as a Methodist minister, I had no awareness of this "tenure." I had observed that Methodists didn't go in for emotionalism, and I was a Methodist. I didn't dare risk a show of feeling.

I took her hand and said, "God bless you. You can go back to your seat now."

She did as I said. I fervently hoped the congregation would quickly forget this incident. For certain, my future appeals to come forward to unite with the church would be less persuasive.

Though my naivete colored my reading of the emotional level of church worship services, continuing experience has corroborated that there is, in fact, an almost intentional effort by Methodists to be nonemotional. Weekly repetitions of ancient creeds — Elizabethan prayers and confessions spliced between lofty hymns of praise — these things do little for the body juices. Intentional or not, the tendency of mainline churches to shy away from displays of feeling is one of the reasons why outbreaks of tongues continue to occur in them.

Dr. Ira Galloway, general secretary for evangelism for the United Methodist Board of Discipleship, and I were discussing the charismatic movement with a group of conference lay leaders from over the southeast. Dr. Galloway told of some difficulties over the tongues phenomenon which he had experienced as a pastor and as a district superintendent. But after sharing with us some of the negative facets of tongues, he went on to give his private assessment of the basis for the continuing interest in tongues.

"The reason, I believe, is the almost total absence of feeling in our church services," he said. "Both theologically and liturgically, our churches are cold and devoid of emotion."

A lawyer and former judge, Dr. Galloway would acknowledge exceptions to any generalization, but his "devoid of emotion" statement does describe a large segment of mainstream Protestantism. As Dr. James F. White has stated, "Protestant worship, for the most part, has been cerebral. It has taken very seriously the importance of words in communicating the gospel and in responding to it. But it has often forgotten that our humanity is not just a matter of disembodied intellects."[2]

Dr. White finds the reasons for this overriding concern with words — the "cerebral movement" — in events concurrent with the Reformation.[3] Specifically, in addition to the theological revolution, there was also a revolution in reading.

The invention of printing from movable type had an impact on worship comparable to the proclamation by

Luther of the priesthood of all believers. Before the day of Gutenberg and the church reformers, public worship was confined to the laity "watching" the mass. The priest read from the Latin and only the rich, well-educated laymen could understand. But within a quarter of a century following Gutenberg's invention, this configuration began to change. The reformers had enough foresight to replace the universal language of worship, Latin, with the national language of the people. (It was 400 years later that the Roman Catholic Church made this accommodation.) This change had a profound effect. The Bible and prayer books became standard fixtures at Protestant worship services. With this development, participation in worship became reading, essentially, and 400 years' practice has entrenched the roles of reading and listening.

Pentecostals, however, have avoided these passive practices. In the churches which my father pastored, the order of worship generally went like this:

As the service began, Papa would ask that the choir be filled. "Choir" referred not to singers, but to the pews behind the pulpit, facing the congregation. Men, women, and children would come forward. If enough didn't come, Papa was not above calling out, "Sister Jones (or Brother Smith), come on up and help us sing." With the choir full, men on one side and ladies on the other, Papa would sit down and the song leader would ask, "Does anyone have a selection?" Someone from the audience or choir would call out the page number of a hymn, the pianist would begin to play, and the song service was under way.

After a few songs, there would be a break for prayer. Papa would ask if anyone had a request for prayer.

From throughout the congregation, requests would be voiced and concerns expressed. Some would stand to speak, others would remain seated, and a few would indicate an unspoken request by raising a hand. Once the concerns had been received, everyone would be invited to come to the altars to kneel and pray. Again, men formed on one side, women on the other. Each request for prayer would be lifted up audibly — sometimes very loudly.

Papa, because of his strong voice and his being the pastor, would "lead" the prayer — that is, he could be heard above everyone else. With rare exceptions, he also always concluded it. After Papa's "Amen," each person would leave the altar and return to his seat.

Then it was time for the offering. The offering plates would be placed on the altar and each person would come up and put in his contribution. People who didn't have regular work or ready cash could take a "pounding slip" out of the offering plate. "Pounding slips" came about this way: The pastor's wife (in this case, my mother) wrote on slips of paper such food items as the parsonage family needed. These slips would be placed in the offering plate before the service. People could pick up a slip as they put in their offering or take out a pounding slip in lieu of giving cash if they had some butter, eggs, potatoes, or perhaps a chicken that they could spare. As a small lad, I sometimes went up and took a pounding slip — an act which left my mother perplexed. At the next service, those who had taken pounding slips would bring the specified item or a substituted commodity and place it in the church entranceway. (In a related practice, parishioners "pounded" a new preacher with gifts of a pound of flour, a pound of coffee, etc.)

Following the offering, there would be a song or two, after which the piano would provide a steady beat as the singers left the choir and marched back to their seats.

Despite the musicians' lack of formal training and the debatable quality of the musical selections, the choir and its singing enhanced the feeling of total participation in the service. The *people* selected the songs and the *people* did the singing. The choir was not a 100-voice spectacle which *entertained* the congregation.

Now came the sermon. Papa would read at least one chapter from the Bible and maybe more. This would be followed by an extensive, extemporaneous prayer. Then, in a loud voice, Papa would begin to preach. Without exception, his sermon included an exposition of the scripture. The sermon, 45 minutes to an hour in duration, would be punctuated by cries from the congregation of "Praise the Lord," "Amen," "Hallelujah," "That's right," or "Yes, Lord." If Papa made a point and nobody responded, he might appeal, "If you believe it, say 'Amen.' " This always prompted a loud chorus of "Amens." (An interesting variation of this occurred while I was preaching in the huge 20,000-member Methodist Pentecostal Church of Santiago, Chile. Periodically, the entire congregation would stand and shout three times in quick succession, *"Gloria a Dios"* or "Glory to God!" It was deafening.)

Following each sermon, whether it was morning or night, midweek or Sunday, Papa issued an invitation for everyone to come to the altar and pray. Finally, the benediction would be offered.

During this same period, mainline Protestant worship

was moving to the opposite pole, according to Dr. White.

"The period of 1920 to 1970 has been the period of respectability for Protestant worship in this country. We got embarrassed out of the fervent 'amen' during sermons or the exclamation of 'hallelujah' at any point in the service. We got accustomed to letting choirs sing the responses, and docilely we read only the words printed for us in the bulletin. Anything spontaneous disappeared and the services became as smooth as butter. Nothing unexpected happened; there were no risks. When the service was broadcast or telecast, it would end very promptly at 11:59:59."[4]

Indeed, this lack of feeling has played a large role in the emergence of the so-called "charismatic movement." The term "charismatic" derives from the Greek word *charisma*, which means "favor" or "gift." In I Corinthians 12-14, Paul used the term to describe the gifts of the Spirit. Though many who consider themselves charismatic do not speak in tongues, the term is popularly associated with those who advocate tongues speaking. According to historian G. Hugh Wamble, the charismatic movement is only one of a number of religious movements spawned in a post-World War II revival of religion:

> These movements emphasized the utter seriousness of Christianity, the inadequacy of nominal Christianity and church membership, the necessity of finding new ways of expressing one's faith and the need of personal assurance. Coming at a time when American denominations were relaxing doctrinal and moral standards and devising church-centered programs, they found an open reception among serious Christians.[5]

The leaders of these movements and their emphases are well known. Examples are Billy Graham, with mass evangelism; Oral Roberts, healing by faith; Glenn Clark, the prayer movement; Ben Johnson, the lay witness mission; and Elton Trueblood, Christian vocations.

The "charismatic movement" (a generic term not associated with a particular individual) uniquely emphasizes the work of the Holy Spirit and an immediacy of communication with God, i.e., an intuitive sensing of God's will. The ideal lifted up is a life that is open to new insights, free to experiment with new forms and methods, and capable of expressing feeling.

But, how beneficial is the expression of feeling in a worship service?

I recall one especially boisterous Pentecostal service at which I was the guest speaker. The opening song service generated so much enthusiasm and emotion that the rest of the service had to be held in abeyance. Men and women were shouting, speaking in tongues, laughing, and crying. While we were waiting for the commotion to subside, the pastor leaned over and said, "Wayne, my people will never need a psychiatrist." If freedom to express one's feelings will keep the psychiatrist away, he was right.

Today's tongues speakers are not frequently subject to criticism for explosive emotionalism, but there was a time when tongues speaking was under a cloud of excess emotionalism. Those who were caught up in that excess were termed "holy rollers." While the term was used derisively, in some degree it accurately described many of the practices around the altars.

Intense seekers of spiritual experiences would sometimes roll back and forth as they sought the blessings of

God. Others would jump up and down, and even run around the church. If the congregation grew unusually demonstrative, the pastor might lead the people in a singing parade around the church — a veritable "Jericho March."

Around the altars, anyone praying or seeking a particular spiritual experience would be exhorted to:

"Let go and let God have his way!"
"Don't quench the Spirit!"
"Open up to the Holy Ghost!"
"Turn your faith loose!"

The evolution of denominations has somewhat refined this robustness, but the emotional base of tongues remains. Many charismatic groups are even more pointedly emotional than their Pentecostal predecessors are.

I recall a rather typical charismatic gathering. The people met in the home of a respected community leader. The ten or twelve people there represented several denominations. After a period of informal conversation, they gravitated into a circle. While holding hands, everyone began praying, quietly at first. Before long, one of the men started to sing in tongues. The "words" were his, but the tune was "Amazing Grace."

Others joined in. While singing, one of the participants lifted her arms. Tears ran down her cheeks and she began talking in tongues, seemingly oblivious of the rest of the group. This triggered other such expressions, and before the evening was over, every regular member of the group had spoken in tongues. Late in the evening, they warmly and affectionately said goodbye after having set the place for the following week's meeting.

This type of emotional expression is, in my thinking, one of the stronger and healthier types. A much more bizarre event took place recently in a midwestern city during a three-day conference on tongues. The conference was sponsored by the Methodist churches of the city and hosted by a prominent church whose new pastor and wife were charismatics.

The special conference speaker was a charismatic, but he didn't practice tongues speaking. Following his address the first evening, the conference broke into small discussion groups.

In one of the groups, the discussion leader inquired about the background of the participants and discovered they were all tongues speakers except for himself and one lady — and she had come to the conference to gain this gift. Except for one Catholic, they were Methodists.

In the group was the pastor of a 600-member Methodist church in a county-seat town a few miles from the conference site. As the group formed into a circle, he remained in a corner facing them. His eyes were closed, his face lifted. His lips were moving, but no sounds came forth.

The discussion leaders had been provided with questions for their groups to consider. The first was, "What possible benefits do you see from speaking in tongues?" In this circle, the first person to respond was an older woman. Quietly she told the group, "Since the outpouring of the Spirit with speaking in tongues in our church, we now have blacks and whites, Protestants and Catholics, people with long hair, young, old, everybody — and we are all worshiping together in the Spirit. I believe tongues can bring us together as Christians . . ."

Before she could finish, the pastor in the corner jumped up and yelled, "That's not right! The Spirit divides!"

Then he told about his experience in the church he was pastoring. Of 600 members, 150 had talked in tongues. With no reticence, he stated that he intended to pull the 150 out and form them into his own Spirit-filled congregation.

When the group leader queried him about his responsibility to the rest of the church, he answered that he was sorry, but they were resisting the work of the Holy Spirit. He was in the same position that Jesus was in with the rich young ruler. (Matthew 19:16-22) When the young ruler couldn't accept the truth about salvation, Jesus had to watch him go away sorrowful. And he, like Jesus, would just have to let the 450 go. The Spirit, he said, was uniting those who believed against those who didn't. To substantiate this, he quoted from Jesus, "I have not come to bring peace on earth; but a sword." (Matthew 10:34)

The group leader reminded him that the point of the story of the rich young ruler had nothing to do with speaking in tongues but instead encouraged giving to the poor and following Christ.

The pastor responded, "That's what we have to do . . . leave whatever we're holding onto and, at whatever the cost, follow Christ. Regardless of how much it hurts."

Now a high school student interjected her testimony. She had received the tongues experience, and in the school hallway the very next day, she felt like speaking in tongues and did.

"It just came out in front of the other students and some teachers. A lot of them were scared and upset, but I felt I had to let go and let the Spirit have his way."

The rest of the group, passive up to now, exploded in praise and prayer, clapping their hands and shouting.

When the group leader tried to restore order, they accused him of trying to quench the Spirit.

The woman who came seeking tongues reiterated her desire, whereupon the tongues-speaking pastor took charge.

He knelt before the lady and asked her, "Do you remember when you were a little girl you used to say, 'Peter Piper picked a peck of pickled peppers; a peck of pickled peppers Peter Piper picked'?"

"Yes, I do," the woman said. "But I always had trouble saying it. I would get the words mixed up."

"Exactly!" he exclaimed. "Now, I'm going to tell you some words just like that. I want you to repeat them after me. You will get them mixed up, too, but don't worry about it. Keep saying them over and over, and soon you will be speaking in tongues. Okay?"

She nodded assent. Then he asked her to stand and to follow him as he walked around the room. Meanwhile, she was to repeat verbatim the following words, "Blessed Jesus, suffering savior, save the sin-sick souls of sinful sinners. We wait, willingly, wantingly, wonderfully, wistfully right now!"

With the group cheering the marching pair, the pastor led the woman around the room repeating the words. Fast, then slow; then fast again. When she began to mix up the words, he sped up the pace. Soon she was standing with her arms lifted high and tears streaming down her face while she repeated strange sounds. To the watching group, the pastor announced that she had received the infilling of the Spirit. What they were hearing, he said, was talking in tongues.

I have described two types of charismatic meetings. A third type is sponsored by the Full Gospel Businessmen's Fellowship International. This group actively and aggressively promotes tongues speaking in non-charismatic churches. Because of their evangelistic purpose, the meetings are designed to reach people who don't speak in tongues. They rely on testimony — from an influential citizen if one is available.

In the introduction, the speaker's success in his business or profession is stressed. Then he offers his testimony. He tells of his past resistance to the work of the Spirit, the questions he faced, the trials, and finally the steps that led to his becoming a tongues speaker. He emphasizes how much his personal — and business — life has improved as a result of this experience.

Before the evening is over, several "messages" in tongues will be given, followed by interpretations. United prayers will be offered. Exclamations of praise will punctuate the service.

The group participation and peer approval which characterize these meetings can be beneficial.

Other psychological patterns in the tongues experience have been described by Dr. John P. Kildahl, who participated in a basically critical study of glossolalia made by a professional research team for the National Mental Health Association. Dr. Kildahl is a practicing psychologist and a member of the faculty of New York Theological Seminary. In *The Psychology of Speaking in Tongues*, which reports the findings of the researchers, Dr. Kildahl relates how an interviewee said he received the tongues experience:

> He had learned a month earlier that his nine-year-old son had leukemia. That made him wonder if there really was a God — a God who affects what goes on in the world. He was

searching. He wondered if life made any sense, and why lovely, innocent little children had to suffer. He wanted to talk about gut-level things: how he could bear the sorrow he knew would be his in the months and years ahead. Could he experience any assurance that there was some real love in the world? His tongues-speaking friends knew what it was to need love and could talk about it freely with him. They prayed together and read from the Bible . . . . They asked if he wanted to receive the gift of the Holy Spirit, and he said he would try. One of the men asked him to imitate his words, *"anee, kitanee ashorum. O, anoramo anayano, Jesu . . ."* and then to kneel and pray. One friend gently laid both his hands on top of his head. The other took the left and right side of his jaw in the thumb and first finger of each hand saying, "Now pray, Jim. Say whatever the Lord gives you to say, and I will move your mouth." *"Abadaba avadaba rehbadaba ramanama . . ."* and the syllables started to come smoothly. Tears flowed down his cheeks as strange words issued from his mouth. He was speaking in tongues.[6]

Dr. Kildahl reported that invariably the tongues speaker was influenced by a strong-personality type, a person who filled a father-type role. "We found no tongue (sic) speaker who was unrelated to a glossolalia authority figure whom he esteemed."[7] The study also revealed that the sound of the tongues expression by the novice resembled the authority figure's expression.

My own experience corroborated these findings. For

me, the influential person was not only a father *type* but a *father* – my own. On those occasions when he spoke in tongues, Papa usually said, *"Hee la mah shun di."* When I began speaking in tongues, I unconsciously included that phraseology precisely.

Dr. Kildahl lists four benefits which those who were interviewed attributed to tongues speaking:

1. There is a stronger sense of identity and self-confidence in interpersonal relationships.

2. There is a greater sense of purpose in life and a deepening of the spiritual quality of life.

3. A sense of boldness is felt in relationships, including business dealings and marriage.

4. There is a conviction that they now matter to God, their neighbors, and to themselves.

"They reported being less annoyed by frustrations, showing greater patience with their families and having a deeper love for mankind in general."[8]

One of the hypotheses originally projected by the research team was that the emotional benefits derived from tongues speaking were not long-lasting – that any initial relief of depression was temporary.

Their extensive examination, however, forced them to conclude just the opposite. After research, testing, and evaluation, they rejected their original hypothesis. "When interviewed and tested a year later, it was found that the tongues-speakers' sense of well-being persisted."[9]

Perhaps an understanding of the psychological dynamics which are at work in tongues differentiates the interpretations of the Pentecostal denominations, on the one hand, and participants in the "charismatic revival" from the historic churches, on the other. Pentecostal groups strongly resist any suggestion that psychological dynamics are at work. For them, speaking in tongues is the evidence of having been baptized by the Holy Spirit — a purely spiritual experience, and an empowerment for witness. It is a gift of God, which he gives of his own free will and pleasure, and it cannot be received by manipulation or psychological techniques. Generally, the Pentecostals would say that those who testify to having received the gift through any of the various devices or mechanisms have been innocently duped and God, out of sympathy, has honored their sincerity — either this, or they simply are imitating the real thing and may or may not know the difference.

That kind of dogmatism is not generally characteristic of the broader charismatic movement. The practices of some charismatics are so divisive as to preclude their assimilation; there is, however, a grudging realization within many churches that charismatics must somehow be accommodated and kept in the mainstream of Christendom.

A growing disenchantment with the present structure and functioning of the institutional church — a disenchantment which is being expressed by both individuals and spiritual movements — prods the mainline churches to accommodate charismatics. If the current trend toward plurality continues into the distant future, the typical metropolitan church may become a "cafeteria of opportunities" — an umbrella under which groups of differing persuasions, including tongues speakers, can meet to share their experiences and deepen their search.

It seems to me that most mainline churches have already moved beyond the point of issuing edicts expelling those members who differ from the majority. As pluralism gains momentum, we can logically expect a renewed emphasis on understanding, mutual respect, and appreciation — even for those who speak in tongues.

5

The Bible Says -

In the award-winning film "The Gospel According to Matthew," Jesus is not a "woman with whiskers"; neither is he a robot untouched by the problems of the will, the mind, and the body. He is not a Jesus with all the rough edges smoothed off. Nor is he made to fit into neat theological categories. He is the Jesus of the gospel!

The Italian director of this film, Pier Pasolini, never had the benefit of theological training nor involvement with the church; yet, his work is exceptionally authentic and revealing. The anomaly of the film is that Pasolini is an avowed communist!

It seems strange that a communist and self-styled atheist could produce a film on Jesus which Christian people of a variety of philosophical and theological persuasions have found powerful and stirring. (Nothing comparable has been produced by Hollywood or the church, either before or since.) How is this possible?

When asked, Pasolini explained that one day in the early 60's, while he was in Rome, he became extremely bored. Vatican Council II was in full swing. The Eternal City was overrun with priests, the religious, and 2,500 bishops. The newspapers, radio, and TV were filled with the events of the Council.

To combat his boredom, Pasolini began to read a New Testament that he found in his hotel room. He started with Matthew. He was profoundly moved. His response was to produce "The Gospel According to Matthew." He remained a communist and atheist, but the simplicity and power of the gospel account had deeply moved him.

One reason why Pasolini could read Matthew and produce such a powerful picture is that he started with few theological presuppositions. He had no denominational axe to grind. He was not concerned with protecting a particular tradition or favored interpretation. In contrast with most Christians, he began with a comparatively clean slate.

When you and I begin to read Matthew, our problem is just the opposite. We were told about Jesus in Sunday School before we ever examined the biblical evidence. We repeated creeds and heard sermons about Jesus which defined him. We sang songs and uttered prayers that described him. The result is that when we approach the Gospel of Matthew, we expect to substantiate the views we've been taught. Instead of the Bible's becoming a "Word of God," spoken to us as we read, we impose upon it preformed ideas which, in reality, are not our own. Because of this conditioning, it is almost impossible for us to have an "open mind" when we read the scripture. Our background of experience and training includes both correct and incorrect information; our attitude is a mixture of prejudice and openness.

This same handicap applies to attempts to understand tongues. There are numerous books "for" tongues or "against" tongues. From pulpits, we've heard some speakers excoriate this experience, others praise it. We've heard scriptures quoted in defense of tongues, and the same scriptures used to condemn tongues. Loaded with this personal experience, we cannot be objective about the meaning of the scriptures. It is most difficult to make our decision strictly on the basis of what "the Bible says." Even in intentional Bible study groups, this difficulty arises.

I knew a group of ladies who met together each week for prayer and Bible study. They had a ground rule: Any comment prefaced by "I think" or "I believe" was unacceptable. Only those statements which started with "The Bible says" were considered appropriate.

While this rule might have contributed an element of discipline to group dynamics, it reflected a fundamental flaw prevalent in many approaches to understanding and interpreting the Bible. For what *I* say "the Bible says" may be different from what *you* say "the Bible says." And very possibly, my understanding may be at odds with the intrinsic meaning of the text.

The Bible — whether read aloud, quoted, or internalized — requires an insight, an interpretation. The interpretation that we make depends on who we are and the experiences that we bring to the biblical record. The more self-conscious we are in our reading, the more significant and insightful the result can be. The more intentional we are in addressing the Bible — that is, the more existential the questions we ask of it — the more beneficial our reading will be. In reality then, the statement "The Bible says" should be expanded to "*I believe* the Bible says." When we tell people the meaning of scripture ("what the Bible says"), we are telling them what the Bible says *as we understand it.* Or, sometimes, *what the Bible means in our lives.*

For this reason, as we examine the biblical treatment of tongues, it is important for us to consider not only the scriptures themselves, but also how we and other people interpret these scriptures.

As an example, in explaining to a Methodist minister some of my views on tongues, I quoted a scripture which I had used many times and which I thought adequately illustrated the point I was attempting to make.

His immediate response was, "But that's not what the scripture means at all."

We got a Bible and checked the verses. Soon we had spread out before us a Greek New Testament, a lexicon, and several commentaries. Eventually, I had to concede that my interpretation of that scripture (though I had held this understanding of it for years) was not well taken. A fresh, in-depth look at the scripture forced me to abandon my viewpoint.

Thus, as you read this chapter, you should be alert to two possible sources of bias. First, *my* choice of scriptures and *my* interpretations of them are colored by my background and experience. Although I have tried to be self-critical, there remains a personal perspective. Second, you need to be conscious of the opinions which *you* already hold concerning tongues. Try to defer adoption of a final interpretation until you have examined the scriptural basis for such a position.

Now, what does the Bible say — that is, what do *I* believe the Bible says about tongues?

First, we can eliminate the Old Testament; there is absolutely no mention of speaking in tongues in any of its thirty-nine books. Of the twenty-seven books of the

New Testament, three specifically mention tongues: Mark, the Acts of the Apostles, and I Corinthians.

In these three books, there are 22 verses in seven chapters which specifically mention speaking in tongues. The words which are translated as "speaking in tongues" are *glossa*, the tongue, and *laleo* or *lalia*, to speak. Though the words are never compounded in the New Testament, today it is a common practice to compound them into *glossolalia*. Through transliteration, tongues speakers are referred to as "glossolaliasts."

Glossolalia is cited once in Mark, four times in Acts, and eighteen times in I Corinthians, for a total of 23 times in the entire Bible (twice in one verse).

In each of the three books, glossolalia is treated differently. In Mark, the mention is brief and unexplained; in Acts, the material is purely descriptive narrative, and I Corinthians teaches about glossolalia and lays down guidelines for its use.

First, the citation in Mark. A very brief mention is made in the disputed last eleven verses of Mark 16, specifically, verse 17: "they will speak in new tongues."

Verses 9-20 of Mark 16 have been challenged by many New Testament scholars. The King James includes them; the Revised Standard Version (which I am using throughout this chapter) makes them a footnote. However, the Revised Standard Version *Catholic Edition* makes them a part of the body of the text as does the new Common Bible. In an appendix, the RSVCE makes this explanatory statement: "As it (verses 9-20) is missing from some important manuscripts, it is possible that Mark did not write it . . . Many think that the original ending was lost at a very early date and that this ending (verses 9-20) was composed at the end of the apostolic period to take its place."[10]

Apart from this being the only gospel which mentions glossolalia, the Gospel of Mark is also unique in that it describes the phenomenon as *new* tongues: "they will speak in new tongues." There is no commentary, only the statement that in the days to come, the new believers shall do many things, including casting out demons, picking up snakes, and healing the sick, as well as speaking in tongues.

The Acts of the Apostles treats glossolalia more substantively. It is Acts that is quoted most often to validate glossolalia as a belief and practice. And it is in Acts that we have the only record of persons actually receiving glossolalia. Each place glossolalia is described as being received, it is related to the infilling of the Holy Spirit. There are thirteen references in Acts either to receiving or being filled with the Holy Spirit. Three of these specifically refer to glossolalia. Four passages refer to a religious experience comparable to the other three, but glossolalia is not hinted. And then there are six references to persons who were full of the Holy Spirit, with no mention made of glossolalia.

Below, all of these verses are quoted, described, and categorized. They are as follows:

1. *Glossolalia specified:*
   a. Pentecost Day — "And they were all filled with the Holy Spirit and began to speak in other tongues, as the Spirit gave them utterance." (Acts 2:4 RSV)
   b. The House of Cornelius at Corinth — "For they heard them speaking in tongues and extolling God." (Acts 10:46 RSV)

c. Disciples of John the Baptist at Ephesus
— "And when Paul had laid his hands
upon them, the Holy Spirit came on
them; and they spoke with tongues and
prophesied." (Acts 19:6 RSV)

2. *Comparable descriptions with no glossolalia suggested:*

a. The revival at Samaria — "Then they laid
their hands on them and they received
the Holy Spirit. Now when Simon saw
that the Spirit was given through the
laying on of the apostles' hands, he offered them money saying, 'Give me also
this power, that any one on whom I lay
my hands may receive the Holy Spirit.' "
(Acts 8:17-19 RSV)

b. Following the trial of Peter and John —
"And when they had prayed, the place in
which they were gathered together was
shaken; and they were all filled with the
Spirit and spoke the word of God with
boldness." (Acts 4:31 RSV)

c. Paul's receiving of the Holy Spirit —
"And laying his hands on him he said,
'Brother Saul, the Lord Jesus who ap-
peared to you on the road by which you
came, has sent me that you may regain
your sight and be filled with the Holy
Spirit.' And immediately something like
scales fell from his eyes and he regained
his sight." (Acts 9:17b, 18a RSV)

d. Following the ouster of Paul and Barna-
bas — "And the disciples were filled with

joy and with the Holy Spirit." (Acts 13:
52 RSV)

3. *Other references to persons being filled
by the Holy Spirit, but with no tongues
suggested:*

a. "Then Peter, filled with the Holy Spirit,
said to them . . ." (Acts 4:8 RSV)

b. "Therefore, brethren, pick out from
among you seven men of good repute,
full of the Holy Spirit and of wisdom
. . ." (Acts 6:3 RSV)

c. "They chose Stephen, a man full of faith
and of the Holy Spirit . . ." (Acts 6:5
RSV)

d. "But he, full of the Holy Spirit, gazed
into heaven . . ." (Acts 7:55 RSV)

e. "For he was a good man, full of the
Holy Spirit and of faith." (Acts 11:24
RSV)

f. "But Saul, who is also called Paul, filled
with the Holy Spirit, looked intently at
him . . ." (Acts 13:9 RSV)

Seen in this context, it is obvious that glossolalia was
not a uniformly accompanying sign. That is not to say
there was no glossolalia; rather, I am underscoring the
fact that glossolalia occurred in the minority of the
instances related in Acts.

Of all of the above, Acts 2:1-4 is without question
the most controversial and requires the most explanation. As noted earlier, the scripture relates that 120 of
the faithful had gathered in Jerusalem to spend ten days
in prayer and praise. On the tenth day, the anticipated
visitation of the Holy Spirit occurred.

One hundred and twenty people speaking in tongues at one time attracted a lot of attention. Since this occurred during one of Israel's most holy periods, the Feast of Weeks, there were Jews from several nations present in Jerusalem. Representatives from seventeen of these countries heard about the tongues commotion and came to see what was happening.

They heard the 120 praising God in seventeen different foreign languages, "And they were amazed and wondered, saying '. . . how is it that we hear, each of us in his own native language?' " (Acts 2:7-8 RSV)

This was not the ecstatic spiritual experience which characterizes glossolalia today, nor were the sounds the same. These people were speaking in *foreign* languages.

This distinction is most important because in none of the other biblical references to glossolalia is speaking in tongues described as a foreign language. As W. G. Putman has noted, except for this one instance, "Glossolalia is everywhere represented as consisting of articulate, significant utterances inspired by the Holy Spirit and employed primarily for worship."[11]

Many persons who practice glossolalia sincerely believe they are uttering some local language or dialect. Others believe that their expressions are in some lost tongue. Yet, researchers have examined hundreds of recorded specimens of glossolalia without ever identifying such sounds with a national language or native dialect. (Of course, many tongues speakers believe that they are speaking in a unique spiritual language which is understood only by God.)

It has been suggested that the miracle described in Acts 2 was not a miracle of *speaking*, but of *hearing*. In other words, the 120 spoke in ecstatic utterances which ordinarily would have been unintelligible because of national or geographical language barriers, but were in this instance comprehended because of a *hearing* miracle which they experienced. Instead of hearing tongues, they heard native languages. This conjecture simply replaces one conundrum with a still larger one.

It is possible that the compiler of Acts intended (judging by his uniformity of word choices) to imply that speaking in foreign languages attended the other tongues outpourings. This is a presumption which is difficult to validate, for the only place in the entire Bible where glossolalia is explicitly referred to as a foreign language is in Acts 2. The other two instances of glossolalia in Acts, chapters 10:46 and 19:6, are more conforming, and neither portrays glossolalia as a foreign language.

In chapter 10, Peter, after inner turmoil and struggle, takes the gospel to the Gentiles. While he was preaching, his listeners began speaking in tongues. "For they heard them speaking in tongues and extolling God." (10:46 RSV) Thereupon, Peter decided they were qualified for water baptism.

In Acts 19, Paul encountered disciples of the late John. He baptized them in the name of the Lord Jesus Christ. Following this, he laid hands on them, and the Holy Spirit came upon them, and they spoke with tongues. "And when Paul had laid his hands upon them, the Holy Spirit came on them; and they spoke with tongues and prophesied." (Acts 19:6 RSV)

Most Pentecostals would insist strenuously that there was a visible manifestation of glossolalia at Samaria. The Samaritans were racially mixed Jews who intermarried with non-Jewish inhabitants during the Exile. The wish of Simon to be able to lay hands on people and have them receive the gift of the Holy Spirit indicates that an unusual physical transformation was manifested following Peter's and John's laying on of hands.

Briefly then, the following conclusions can be drawn about the Acts accounts of tongues:

1. *Everyone in each of the three worshiping groups is reported to have experienced tongues.* Whether the group is the 120 in Jerusalem, the friends of Cornelius assembled in Corinth, or the disciples of John the Baptist at Ephesus, no one was left out; everybody present spoke in tongues. A modern analogy would be a church where no one speaks in tongues until a visiting tongues-speaking minister comes in and shares his beliefs, whereupon everyone present starts speaking in tongues.

2. *The recipients are passive in receiving tongues.* They don't initiate the tongues or sustain their continued expression. Rather, through an irresistible act, God, the Holy Spirit, decides when, where, and how long.

3. *Tongues does not uniformly accompany the infilling of the Spirit.* Because of this variation, it is difficult to support the contention (1) that to be filled with the Spirit requires speaking in tongues, or (2) that tongues is the evidence of having been baptized with the Holy Spirit.

4. *Each reception of tongues is received by a distinctly different group.* First, the Jews (Acts 2); second, Gentiles, who were mainly

Romans and Greeks (Acts 10); and third, an isolated group of followers of John the Baptist, who may have been early followers of Christ (Acts 19).

5. *Tongues speaking is the miracle which demonstrates and validates the ushering in of the Spirit.* According to the gospels, Christ promised that after his death and resurrection, his followers would have another Counselor. The Holy Spirit would take Christ's place. In the same way that the gospels of Matthew and Luke record miraculous happenings regarding the birth of Jesus, Acts tells of the ushering in of the Holy Spirit and of an appropriate accompaniment — namely, speaking in tongues. The gospels recount the stir caused by the birth of Jesus, and Acts tells how the introduction of the Holy Spirit created a comparable commotion.

6. *In only one instance (Acts 2) is tongues speaking represented as a foreign language.* None of the other accounts in Acts suggest this. As will be seen in the next chapter, I Corinthians clearly states that tongues speaking is not a language understood by men.

7. *There is no single, prescribed tongues reception.* Tongues variously follows ten days of prayer, preaching, and water baptism.

In summary, Acts is a descriptive narrative. It tells of the Spirit's coming to the early church and it relates how the members spoke in tongues.

If Acts were the only biblical resource for understanding the phenomenon of tongues, there would be no scriptural guidelines for dealing with its use or misuse. When one of the first churches to be established in biblical times became scandalous in its misuse of tongues, an emissary was sent to the Apostle Paul to resolve the problems. Paul's response, contained in I Corinthians, provides a distinctively different perspective from that of the Acts.

6
"Can Tongues Help the Church?"

It is interesting to examine how the first church leader to confront abuses with glossolalia dealt with it. The leader? The Apostle Paul. The place? Corinth. The time? About 56 A.D.

If you have heard of problems in churches, they are probably mild compared to those of the Church of Christ at Corinth. The members were racked by flagrant excesses in virtually every area. Only four or five years after Paul founded the church, the members divided into warring factions. Their differences resulted in court suits, which were disgracing them in the eyes of non-Christians.

There were serious lapses in morality, including incest and the use of the pagan temple prostitutes. The Lord's Supper had become repugnant. Church decorum was totally lacking.

Strangely enough, their lapses were combined with spiritual zeal, and this zeal itself proved troublesome. Their desire to have all the gifts of the Spirit totally disrupted the services of public worship. One of the greatest problems was their abuse of the gift of tongues. No one could attempt to communicate to the congregation without several others (especially the women) jumping up to speak in tongues. There was no order, no courtesy. The services were scandalous. No one's leadership was respected.

Finally, a delegation from the church met with the Apostle Paul.

Paul's letter to the church, which we call I Corinthians, devotes three of its sixteen chapters to delineating the appropriate use of glossolalia. These three chapters — 12, 13, and 14 — are the only ones in the entire Bible which give any guidance for understanding, or for dealing with, the problems caused by the misuse of tongues.

Generally, interpretations of these chapters run to either of two extremes: Tongues speakers ignore most of the negative statements, while those who do not speak in tongues read only the negative. One of the problems has been the tendency to take verses out of context. For example, within one chapter you can lift out verses to "prove" your position, whichever side you're on.

"Now I want you all to speak in tongues" can be interpreted as blanket approval of glossolalia by Paul. But consider also, *"I would rather speak five words with my mind, in order to instruct others, than ten thousand words in a tongue."* That seems to deprecate glossolalia. Neither of these verses can be taken out of context and still convey what the whole of Paul's letter intended.

To get a clear meaning of these three chapters, specific usages need to be understood. One important term is Paul's constant underscoring of the importance of prophecy.

Unfortunately, "prophecy" has come to have a connotation of one who *foretells* the future. But to Paul, in the middle of the first century, it primarily meant one who engaged in *forthtelling* — that is, one who applied the Christ event to the life and times in which the people were living.[12] Prophets and their prophecies would be comparable to today's preacher and his sermon, except that in Paul's day they evidently had more than one prophecy in a given service.

Another phrase which poses difficulty of understanding is Paul's insistence that messages in tongues during church services must be interpreted. (Note that it is *interpreted*, not *translated*.) What was interpretation? Briefly, it meant that if someone spoke in tongues during a worship service, it would be necessary to have someone else publicly interpret the meaning of what was said; otherwise, nobody, including the speaker himself, would understand it. In essence, then, interpretation was a short sermon. And the interpretation was another form of prophecy, or forthtelling.

Today, in charismatic and Pentecostal services, the leader or pastor oftentimes will interpret the tongues messages. The honest ones do not pretend to have understood the language in the way a translator does. Rather, the interpreters feel that as they speak, they will be given special insight to relay to the people what God has said to them. The interpretation usually winds up being an exhortation to deeper commitment, punctuated with "Yea, I say unto you . . ."

Now to examine the three chapters themselves. Since they are not among the most frequently read chapters, they are printed here in their entirety, each of them followed by commentary.

I Corinthians 12

Now concerning spiritual gifts, brethren, I do not want you to be uninformed. 2You know that when you were heathen, you were led astray to dumb idols, however you may have been moved. 3Therefore I want you to understand that no one speaking by the Spirit of God ever says "Jesus be cursed!" and no one can say "Jesus is Lord" except by the Holy Spirit.

4Now there are varieties of gifts, but the same Spirit; 5and there are varieties of service, but the same Lord; 6and there are varieties of working, but it is the same God who inspires them all in every one. 7To each is given the manifestation of the Spirit for the common good. 8To one is given through the Spirit the utterance of wisdom, and to another the utterance of knowledge according to the same Spirit, 9to another faith by the same Spirit, to another gifts of healing by the one Spirit, 10to another the working of miracles, to another prophecy, to another the ability to distinguish between spirits, to another various kinds of tongues, to another the interpretation of tongues. 11All these are inspired by one and the same Spirit who apportions to each one individually as he wills.

12For just as the body is one and has many members, and all the members of the body, though many, are one body, so it is with Christ. 13For by one Spirit we were all baptized into one body — Jews or Greeks, slaves or free — and all were made to drink of one Spirit.

14For the body does not consist of one member but of many. 15If the foot should say, "Because I am not a hand, I do not belong to the body," that would not make it any less a part of the body. [16]And if the ear should say, "Because I am not an eye, I do not belong to the body," that would not make it any less a part of the body. [17]If the whole body were an eye, where would be the hearing? If the whole body were an ear, where would be the sense of smell? [18]But as it is, God arranged the organs in the body, each one of them, as he chose. [19]If all were a single organ, where would the body be? [20]As it is, there are many parts, yet one body. [21]The eye cannot say to the hand, "I have no need of you," nor again the head to the feet, "I have no need of you." [22]On the contrary, the parts of the body which seem to be weaker are indispensable, [23]and those parts of the body which we think less honorable we invest with the greater honor, and our unpresentable parts are treated with greater modesty, [24]which our more presentable parts do not require. But God has so adjusted the body, giving the greater honor to the inferior part, [25]that there may be no discord in the body, but that the members may have the same care for one another. [26]If one member suffers, all suffer together; if one member is honored, all rejoice together.

[27]Now you are the body of Christ and individually members of it. [28]And God has appointed in the church first apostles, second prophets, third teachers, then workers of miracles, then healers, helpers, administrators, speakers in various kinds of tongues. [29]Are all apostles? Are all prophets? Are all teachers? Do all work miracles? [30]Do all possess gifts of healing? Do all speak with tongues? Do all interpret? [31]But earnestly desire the higher gifts.

And I will show you a still more excellent
way. (RSV)

The real problem Paul is struggling with in this
chapter is inappropriate elevation of the gifts of the
Spirit. Using the analogy of the body, he shows that
there are many parts, none unimportant and all related
to the whole.

Three times, Paul makes mention of either the gifts
or the holders of these gifts (8-10, 28, and 29-30).
Without exception, tongues and the interpretation of
tongues are listed last. Paul assigns a relatively low value
to tongues.

One of the very real problems in relating to charismatics who testify to the importance of glossolalia in
their lives is the tendency to reverse the order given here.
It's a form of religious myopia. Glossolalia is the event
nearest to them, and, consequently, the only one they
see. The church, its ministry, other Christians, and the
gospel itself are seen only through the lens of glossolalia.

Rather than glossolalia's being accepted as one of the
minor gifts of the Spirit, it becomes *the* norm for
Christian self-understanding. One clear intent of chapter
12 is to place not only glossolalia, but all the gifts which
Paul lists, within the context of the whole gospel. It is
against the gift of God proclaimed in Christ that the
gift of tongues must finally be compared, according to
Chapter 12.

Lest, however, that comparison not be convincing
enough, Paul offers in chapter 13 another criterion for
evaluation. Though this chapter is a masterpiece of
writing, it should be read within context. That context
includes an attempt by Paul to control the rampant
glossolalia in Corinth.

I Corinthians 13

If I speak in the tongues of men and of angels, but have not love, I am a noisy gong or a clanging cymbal. 2And if I have prophetic powers, and understand all mysteries and all knowledge, and if I have all faith, so as to remove mountains, but have not love, I am nothing. 3If I give away all I have, and if I deliver my body to be burned, but have not love, I gain nothing.

4Love is patient and kind; love is not jealous or boastful; 5it is not arrogant or rude. Love does not insist on its own way; it is not irritable or resentful; 6it does not rejoice at wrong, but rejoices in the right. 7Love bears all things, believes all things, hopes all things, endures all things.

8Love never ends; as for prophecy, it will pass away; as for tongues, they will cease; as for knowledge, it will pass away. 9For our knowledge is imperfect and our prophecy is imperfect; 10but when the perfect comes, the imperfect will pass away. 11When I was a child, I spoke like a child, I thought like a child, I reasoned like a child; when I became a man, I gave up childish ways. 12For now we see in a mirror dimly, but then face to face. Now I know in part; then I shall understand fully, even as I have been fully understood. 13So faith, hope, love abide, these three; but the greatest of these is love. (RSV)

As Paul begins comparing the gifts of the Spirit with love, the very first gift he calls attention to is tongues. Whether tongues be considered a language of men or of angels, it is merely an obnoxious percussion instrument *if it fails to possess love*. It's a band member who is beating the gong and striking the cymbal, totally oblivious of everyone else. It's a spiritual ego trip under the guise of superior insight; it's a special "wisdom" that can ignore both divinely ordained leadership and the concerns of others.

When Jesus was asked which commandment was the greatest, he quoted from the Torah: "Hear, O Israel: The Lord our God is one Lord; and you shall love the Lord your God with all your heart, and with all your soul, and with all your might." (Deuteronomy 6:4-5) Then, he added that the second commandment, ". . . you shall love your neighbor as yourself" (Leviticus 19: 18), was equally important with the first.

Paul now gives the same admonition. His eloquent statement is an appeal for self-giving love – a love which finds fulfillment and satisfaction through the giving of one's time, talent, and energy to others.

In essence, Paul is saying, "Keep clanging away by speaking in tongues if you must, but don't delude yourselves into thinking that tongues is *that* important – not without a deep and abiding love for others."

Now in Chapter 14, Paul turns to specific instructions on the use of tongues. Lest there be any misunderstanding about the importance he attaches to what he is saying, he summarizes it with these words: "If any one thinks that he is a prophet, or spiritual, he should acknowledge that what I am writing to you is a command of the Lord. If any one does not recognize this, he is not recognized."

I Corinthians 14

Make love your aim, and earnestly desire the spiritual gifts, especially that you may prophesy. 2For one who speaks in a tongue speaks not to men but to God; for no one understands him, but he utters mysteries in the Spirit. 3On the other hand, he who prophesies speaks to men for their upbuilding and encouragement and consolation. 4He who speaks in a tongue edifies himself, but he who prophesies edifies the church. 5Now I want you all to speak in tongues, but even more to prophesy. He who prophesies is greater than he who speaks in tongues, unless some one interprets, so that the church may be edified.

6Now brethren, if I come to you speaking in tongues, how shall I benefit you unless I bring you some revelation or knowledge or prophecy or teaching? 7If even lifeless instruments, such as the flute or the harp, do not give distinct notes, how will any one know what is played? 8And if the bugle gives an indistinct sound, who will get ready for battle? 9So with yourselves; if you in a tongue utter speech that is not intelligible, how will any one know what is said? For you will be speaking into the air. 10There are doubtless many different languages in the world, and none is without meaning; 11but if I do not know the meaning of the language, I shall be a foreigner to the speaker and the speaker a foreigner to me. 12So with yourselves; since you are eager for manifestations of the Spirit, strive to excel in building up the church.

13Therefore, he who speaks in a tongue should pray for the power to interpret. 14For if I pray in a tongue, my spirit prays but my mind is unfruitful. 15What am I to do? I will pray with the spirit and I will pray with the mind also; I will sing with the spirit and I will sing with the mind also. 16Otherwise, if you bless with the spirit, how can any one in the position of an outsider say the "Amen" to your thanksgiving when he does not know what you are saying? 17For you may give thanks well enough, but the other man is not edified. 18I thank God that I speak in tongues more than you all; 19nevertheless, in church I would rather speak five words with my mind, in order to instruct others, than ten thousand words in a tongue.

20Brethren, do not be children in your thinking; be babes in evil, but in thinking be mature. 21In the law it is written, "By men of strange tongues and by the lips of foreigners will I speak to this people, and even then they will not listen to me, says the Lord." 22Thus, tongues are a sign not for believers but for unbelievers, while prophecy is not for unbelievers but for believers. 23If, therefore, the whole church assembles and all speak in tongues, and outsiders or unbelievers enter, will they not say that you are mad? 24But if all prophesy, and an unbeliever or outsider enters, he is convicted by all, he is called to account by all, 25the secrets of his heart are disclosed; and so, falling on his face, he will worship God and declare that God is really among you.

26What then, brethren? When you come together, each one has a hymn, a lesson, a revelation, a tongue, or an interpretation. Let all things be done for edification. 27If any speak in a tongue, let there be only two or at most three, and each in turn; and let one interpret. 28But if there is no one to interpret, let each of them keep silence in church and speak to himself and to God. 29Let two or three prophets speak, and let the others weigh what is said. 30If a revelation is made to another sitting by, let the first be silent. 31For you can all prophesy one by one, so that all may learn and all be encouraged; 32and the spirits of prophets are subject to prophets. 33For God is not a God of confusion but of peace.

As in all the churches of the saints, 34the women should keep silence in the churches. For they are not permitted to speak, but should be subordinate, as even the law says. 35If there is anything they desire to know, let them ask their husbands at home. For it is shameful for a woman to speak in church. 36What! Did the word of God originate with you, or are you the only ones it has reached?

37If any one thinks that he is a prophet, or spiritual, he should acknowledge that what I am writing to you is a command of the Lord. 38If any one does not recognize this, he is not recognized. 39So, my brethren, earnestly desire to prophesy, and do not forbid speaking in tongues; 40but all things should be done decently and in order. (RSV)

It is impossible to read this chapter and conclude that Paul denies the reality of tongues. He personally testifies to practicing it himself — "I thank God that I speak in tongues more than you all" (Verse 18). He even says, "Now, I want you all to speak in tongues" (5). And lest anyone try to set aside the reality of this experience, he expressly states, "Do not forbid speaking in tongues" (39).

Yet, there are a great many qualifications and guidelines to be applied if the use of tongues is to be appropriate. First, Paul states that tongues is not as important as prophecy (5b). Also, if tongues is spoken in church, there should always be an interpretation. This interpretation would be another form of prophecy.

Second, Paul underscores that the primary benefits accrue to the individual who is doing the tongues speaking. No one else can understand him, for he speaks to God. Verses 18 and 19 speak to this point specifically. How can Paul, on the one hand, boast of being a bigger tongues speaker than these people, then turn right around and declare that five words spoken by the mind are more important than 10,000 words spoken in tongues?

It's rather simple if the little phrase "in church" is noted. In church, tongues is unimportant. It takes 10,000 words of tongues to equal five rationally spoken words – a ratio of 2,000 to 1. That's a rather devastating indictment of tongues when practiced in church.

Yet, Paul still claims to be the greatest tongues speaker of all. One possible resolution is that Paul is redirecting the importance of tongues from the level of public display to the dimension of personal edification in private.

Third, Paul strives to bring a sense of responsibility and decorum to worship. He insists that worship must be designed to benefit those who are not Christians and do not understand such things as speaking in tongues. He concludes his commentary on tongues by saying, "All things should be done decently and in order" (40).

To generalize further, there are three questions which bring into focus the parameters of glossolalia as discussed by Paul in these chapters.

1. Do tongues meet the test of Christian love?

Christian love is not placid, passive, or ineffectual. It is the love which is incarnate in Jesus – the love which revolutionized the Roman world. It's the love expressed in Gandhi which broke the yoke of British imperialism for India. It's the love presented in Martin Luther King which marched into the strongholds of American racial prejudice and exposed a sick nation. Christian love is a love which is powerful. As Reinhold Niebuhr has said: "Anyone who incarnates the strategy of love as Jesus did meets the resistance and incites the passions of human society. The respectabilities of any human society are based upon moral compromises and every community is as anxious to defend these compromises against the prophet who presents some higher moral logic as against the criminal who imperils the structure from below."[13]

The harvest reaped from planting that kind of love never ends. Its benefits reverberate like ripples from a stone thrown into a placid lake. Without that kind of love, tongues is sounding brass and tinkling cymbals. Held up against that banner, tongues is a momentary fancy, an ephemeral form that will soon pass away. Matched against that understanding, *tongues* is an expression of childish ways, but *love* is an expression of Christian maturity.

Does speaking in tongues meet the test of love? At Corinth it didn't, and for many divided churches around the world it still hasn't.

This eventuality does not preclude its *ever* happening; but judging by its nature, it's doubtful that it will, in most instances.

There are two reasons for this. One, to seek tongues is to seek to benefit self. In whatever form the desire for tongues is expressed, it is a self-serving experience. As Dave Wilkerson, the well-known minister to addicts, has reported, tongues takes the place of narcotics for many former addicts.[14] For many charismatic Christians, tongues is a spiritual high.

The second reason that tongues fails to meet the test of love is that, once it is received, it is of benefit only to the recipient. It is for personal edification. It is not an experience that can be truly shared with others. It seldom turns one to persons who are in need; more often, it turns the recipient either inward or to others of the same conviction.

2. Does tongues help people to come to terms with themselves – that is, to love themselves?

Any objective reading of I Corinthians 12-14 will result in a conclusion that Paul does recognize some benefits in tongues speaking. But it is in the context of private devotions and for personal edification that tongues is recommended.

Within this understanding, tongues can be seen as an aid in praying to God: "For one who speaks in tongues speaks not to men but to God." (I Cor. 14:2 RSV) It can be a source of personal edification: "He who speaks in a tongue edifies himself." (14:4 RSV)

And if kept within boundaries of common sense and propriety, tongues can be a source of emotional release and an aid against depression. In this sense, then, tongues can meet the test of aiding self-understanding.

Yet, even this is said "left-handedly." For people with good emotional health and a sense of personal worth who experience tongues will reflect those same characteristics after tongues. Concomitantly, those persons with varying degrees of emotional instability will, it seems to me, only reflect that insecurity more acutely upon receiving tongues. Given, however, an affirming group of peers who understand those problems, tongues could conceivably be a resource for release of tension and pent-up feelings.

A hostile person with deeply suppressed fears and anger will retain these negative feelings even after he talks in tongues. He may now, however, divert his hostility to those who don't believe the way he does.

The third test of glossolalia is:

3. Does it contribute to the overall witness of faith to the Christ event?

One of the ironies which blemish the Christian religion is that where the most religious zeal is displayed, the mission of Jesus is often of least concern.

Upon beginning his ministry, Jesus stated his mission in this way: "The Spirit of the Lord is upon me, because he has anointed me to preach good news to the poor. He has sent me to proclaim release to the captives and recovering of sight to the blind, to set at liberty those who are oppressed." (Luke 4:18 RSV)

Using the same norms as guides, the missional imperative upon the Christian is to be Christ for his neighbor, to represent Christ to others at the point of their need.

While Colin Morris was deeply involved in the ecumenical struggle, he was also serving as president of the United Church of Zambia. One day, a little black man dropped dead at his door. On autopsy, a pathologist found only a few strands of grass in his stomach. Morris said, "Little men with shrunken bellies call the church's bluff."[15]

The self-serving nature of tongues made it necessary for Paul to emphasize the importance of prophecy over tongues, for without interpretation, tongues never pointed to Christ. It never proclaimed the relevance of faith unless it was restated in understandable language.

Seek tongues? Surely, but only within the context of seeking more resources to re-present the Christ who stands against *all* forms of tyranny — whether it be a flag-wrapped chauvinism which condones the obliteration of little nations, the mindless drivel that polarizes brother against brother, or the hate that would see people starve rather than share. If tongues can participate in *that process* of evangelism and service, then tongues should be sought.

Some time ago, I had the opportunity to introduce Oral Roberts to Ben Johnson, the creator of the Lay Witness Mission. Johnson is a Methodist minister and director of The Institute of Church Renewal, Atlanta, Georgia. His full energies are given to the creation of ways and means for renewing the church. Because of this commitment, he maintains a basic openness to new and different ways of articulating the faith, and he sought Roberts' views concerning the task of renewing the church.

During the conversation, the subject of glossolalia came up. Roberts is an enthusiastic adherent of glossolalia. Though Johnson is generally affirmative of those who witness to the importance of this experience in their lives, he personally does not practice it. Johnson commented that many who are committed to renewing the church view the inappropriate use of glossolalia as a serious problem. Johnson articulated this concern, then stated his own understanding of glossolalia.

Roberts indicated that he understood Johnson's position. Then he made some surprising statements: First, he reported that at one time he had investigated personally every instance that had come to his attention of a Methodist preacher's advocating glossolalia and thereby getting into trouble — encountering problems with his church members, district superintendent, or bishop. And without exception, according to Roberts, the preacher had been unwise in his practices; moreover, the minister misunderstood what the Bible says about glossolalia. In other words, the *methods* of the preachers had gotten them in trouble, not the glossolalia itself.

Second, Roberts advised: "Ben, if you ever talk in tongues, don't tell anyone about it!"

The counsel seemed out of character coming as it did from Roberts, whose life story and charismatic experiences are known by thousands. Roberts explained his admonition this way: "Those who have been identified with charismatic groups all their lives can speak about their experiences and not create antagonism. But if a person such as you were suddenly to claim the gift of the Holy Spirit, it would create enormous conflict, for you would be wearing it as a badge of identification, something to set you apart from others. So if you get it, don't tell anyone."

7
From Across the Tracks to Downtown

In *The Social Teaching of the Church*, Ernst Troelstch describes two basic types of organized religious groups.[16] One of these is the *sect* type. The other is the *church* type.

The members of the sect-type groups separate themselves from both non-Christians and those Christians who do not believe as they do. They live a self-denying life. They refuse to go along with the crowd; they defy social convention. Instead, they devote themselves to seeking personal holiness, to overcoming the desires of the body, and to associating only with those of like mind.

In this way, sect-type churches seek to be beacons unto the world, lights shining in the darkness. And their witness is exemplified by their life-style. They have noticeably different social patterns and living habits which are distinct from the masses. They refuse to be tainted by the sinful acts of their fellowmen. They are *in* the world, but not *of* the world.

Identifiable groups which currently fit into the pattern described above (although some are evolving out of it) are not only the Pentecostal groups such as the

Assemblies of God, Pentecostal Holiness, and Church of God, but also such diverse groups as the Church of the Nazarene, Jehovah's Witness, Seventh Day Adventist, Mennonite Brethren, the Amish, and the Jesus People.

Troelstch's other category, the church type, holds that to win others, you must *identify* with them. To raise the quality of life and to improve social standards demand *participation*. To refuse to become involved in the processes of human society — processes which determine the character of that society — is to be irresponsible. This is God's world, and man has been given dominion over and responsibility for this world.

Within this self-understanding, it is important for the church to gain social recognition. Its membership and leadership should include politicians, educators, leading businessmen, and other influential persons. (The corollary of this is the affinity of such leaders for socially recognized churches.) This social consciousness is exemplified by the importance which the church types attach to the election of their members to high public offices. Another reflection is the predilection of some denominations to compare their church governments with the national government — for example, the United Methodists are fond of calling their Judiciary Council "Methodism's Supreme Court."

These two types of groups — sect and church — could be labeled the "salt type" and the "leaven type." The salt (sect) type never loses its distinctiveness; it always stands out. Its essential composition ensures that it will never lose its own identity while attempting to affect others.

The leaven (church) type, however, does not see itself so radically defined or sharply delineated. Rather, by participating in and being a part of the social process, it seeks to raise the level of the whole of human events.

While the sect type risks having little impact on social processes, without question it does retain its identity. Conversely, the church type assures for itself an effective voice in the events of the world, but it runs the risk of losing the distinctive quality of its witness.

In the history of most Protestant denominations, there has been an evolution from sect type to church type. One of the best examples is the very church from which Pentecostalism sprang — the Methodist Church.

Originally, John Wesley intended for his Methodists to be an "evangelistic order" within the Church of England.[17] In England, Methodism did not break ranks until after Wesley's death, but in America, geographical separation, lack of communication, and the Revolutionary War catalyzed the formation of a separate religious body.

The distinctive theological contribution of John Wesley was his unique interpretation and adaptation of the doctrine of Christian perfection. This doctrine, by the time it was reinterpreted on the American frontier, was known as the experience of "entire sanctification." That branch of Methodism which aspired to this experience and professed it became known as "holiness people." And in the latter part of the nineteenth century, there was no group more socially rigid and evangelistic about their beliefs and codes than the sanctified saints of Methodism. They fulfilled all the criteria of a sect-type church.

The controversy over their interpretation of Christian perfection resulted in a schism in Methodism which eventually saw the splintering off of scores of groups who formed their own denominations. At least 100 denominations can be traced to this controversy.[18] During the period 1893-1900, twenty-three holiness denominations were formed.[19] The largest of that group to survive to this day is the Church of the Nazarene.[20] Most of these groups retained their Methodist heritage — in doctrine, polity, and practice.

The exodus had a greater impact than its numbers would suggest. No more than 100,000 of the four million members of the Methodist Church left over the holiness controversy.[21] Yet, a decisive identity struggle gripped Methodism after the exodus of the holiness groups. Those who were left behind were unable to reinterpret the Wesleyan theological contribution of Christian perfection in any way other than the way that the departed entire sanctification advocates had interpreted it. This inability led them to throw the baby out with the bath water. The result was a theological casualness in Methodist churches which has few denominational counterparts.

By the turn of the century, all traces of sect-type identity had been excised from Methodism. There were occasional attempts to reintroduce the holiness emphasis into the church, but they were uniformly insignificant. *Methodism was a church type!*

How a church goes from the sect type to the church type can be explained by historical processes. In *A Study of History*, Arnold Toynbee analyzed the rise and fall of civilization, and his study illuminates the dynamics of the church process, also.

Toynbee explained that the changing cast of world powers can be understood in terms of cycles. Just as plants have a cycle, so do civilizations. A flower sprouts from a small seed, develops as a young plant, matures with vigorous buds, then breaks out in beautiful and rich blooms, and finally becomes an old and dying flower.

His predecessor in thought, Oswald Spengler, compares this cyclical process to the seasons of the year. In the spring of its life, a civilization may be small and unnoticed. But with a young and vigorous citizenry, it can grow to strength and power. However, the results of success contain the seeds of destruction. Eventually, this civilization too will fall into decay and be surpassed by another. "The culture may continue as a mere *civilization*, which preserves the outer framework but is without the creative spirit."[22]

A church may start as a group of people who are insignificant in number and in wealth, education, and social standing. But if they are sincere and honest, and believe in God's blessings upon their efforts — these motives and the expression of these motives will change their status. Their honesty and trustworthiness cause them to be promoted on the job. Their thrift results in savings. Another way of saying it is, "Good religion makes good business."

This typology of sect type and church type is not rigid and unchangeable. In fact, the Pentecostal churches represent a classic example of the evolution from sect to church type.

Without question, the Pentecostal churches were initially a sect type and most of them remain sect type, but they have begun the process of change. In the past, their strong social codes automatically identified them as "different." Pentecostals did not smoke, drink, use profane language, play cards, dance, attend motion pictures, or go swimming with members of the opposite sex. The women did not cut their hair. They did not wear any sort of make-up, short-sleeved dresses or short skirts, or rings, necklaces, earrings, or other jewelry. To do any of this was to be "worldly."

While other boys wore shorts in gym class, Pentecostal children wore trousers. When other little boys wore short pants, I wore my long stockings — or if my stockings were too worn, rather than wear anklets (worldly!) I went without socks.

When Mother's hair grew past her knees, it pulled so heavily on her head that she had headaches. It was a matter of deep internal struggle for her to decide whether or not to shorten it, for the Bible specifically said, "If a woman have long hair, it is a glory to her." (I Cor. 11:15) Her final decision was to shorten it only a little bit.

At night, Mother always put it into a single braid. During one of our frequent moves, this time to a small farm, a snake was found in a fireplace. The discovery unnerved Mother. That night, the whole house was awakened to her screams as she frantically tried to get a "snake" out of her bed. The "snake" was her braid of hair!

Mother's younger sister once rebelliously declared that she was going to cut off her hair, regardless of the consequences. She told her mother she'd rather have a whipping and short hair than long hair and no whipping. Grandmother told her it would be a whipping all right — one whipping a day until her hair grew back out!

During World War II, my fourth-grade class was preparing to see "Lassie, Come Home." A special matinee showing had been arranged at a local theater. Each child had to obtain approval from his parents. In my family, none of us children had ever gone to a picture show before, but because the story was about a dog, my parents approved my going (including the expenditure of ten cents).

When the anticipated day came, we loaded into the school bus. Everyone was excited, but none more than the Pentecostal preacher's son. As we waited for the bus to depart, someone yelled out, "Come on, Jimmy."

I looked out the window and saw Jimmy standing forlornly on the sidewalk. The bus pulled away, leaving Jimmy standing there, alone.

I knew Jimmy well. His father, like mine, was a Pentecostal preacher, except he had a much smaller church in a much poorer part of town. Jimmy's father had refused to let him go.

When I got home that evening, I excitedly told my brother and sister about the beautiful collie dog which could do about everything. I mentioned that Jimmy was the only one who couldn't go.

My brother told me that Jimmy's church didn't believe in picture shows. My sister responded that ours didn't either. That produced a conflict which we could not resolve among ourselves. I was just glad that I hadn't been the only one to remain behind.

Very few persons, children or adults, want to be like Jimmy — one person, standing alone, separate and different from everyone else because of the beliefs he holds. Yet, it is this willingness to be different that produced the Pentecostal denominations of the twentieth century.

This whole genre of social behavior seemed counterproductive at first. Until the middle of the century, Pentecostals were socially insignificant. They were the butt of jokes and were ridiculed as "holy rollers." They did not inspire interest or confidence except among the poor, the uneducated, and the disfranchised. In principle, First Church, on the corner of Main Street, U.S.A., was open to the down-and-out; in practice, however, it was the Pentecostals who evidenced concern for them and aggressively evangelized them.

The honesty, hard work, trustworthiness, and ethical principles preached and taught in the Pentecostal churches began to result in increased productivity and thrift. Children of uneducated parents now were encouraged to pursue better training. Higher pay and a willingness to save made for more flexibility in living accommodations, clothing, and cars. The socioeconomic level rose significantly.

The church buildings reflected this emergence. Storefront churches were abandoned, and brick sanctuaries arose. The other-side-of-the-tracks churches began to move into the suburbs. The once simple and informal services began to resemble worship in the mainline churches. There were robed choirs and anthems, multiple staffs, and ministry specialists.

The net result was that by the middle of the century, Pentecostals had begun to take on the accouterments of progress. Their young ministers were becoming educated. A growing number of laymen were entering professional and business fields. Their financial worth was increasing.

With this came a loosening of the strict social codes. Girls and women were permitted shorter hair, make-up, jewelry, and fashionable clothing. Other walls which made for separatism began to fall. The identity tags of being a small, unprogressive bunch of "holy rollers" began to fall off. The increasing numbers of Pentecostals and their evangelistic effectiveness were more and more to be reckoned with. Fewer and fewer second and third-generation Pentecostals were inclined to pursue aggressively the codes of yesteryear. Those who did were mostly in the rural areas.

To illustrate the "new" version of the Pentecostal Church, let me describe my recent visit to a large and growing church in the most attractive suburban area of Tulsa.

When I entered, a smiling usher wearing a boutonniere directed me to a beautiful pew with an upholstered seat. I was kept quite comfortable by central air conditioning. Indirect lighting rested my eyes. The robed choir presented special music, with organ accompaniment. Prayer was offered from the pulpit.

Then the pastor, who is a college and seminary graduate with good diction and flawless grammar, talked about the sins of the world and the flesh. (Admittedly a throwback.) He threw several punches at "nominal" churches, their materialism, and their concern for the things of the world. He said all this with a straight face, even though he himself has two cars, one of them a new Buick, which he parks in the two-car garage of his four-bedroom home. Since most of the sermon was taken to be directed at "others," there was little need for a personal response from those who were present.

The sermon had changed less than the environment. In content, it retained much of the character of the sermons of the Pentecostal founders, who were adamantly convinced of their rightness and sharply defensive against the "worldly and normal churches." But in terms of presentation, there remained little of the verve and vitality which characterized early Pentecostal preachers. The words were much the same, but their relevance had been eroded by the changing times.

A closing hymn was sung, a perfunctory altar call made. Promptly at 12 noon, we were dismissed.

The performance was "up front." The participation of the audience was limited to standing, sitting, and standing again. This service, while it was less sophisticated and perhaps not so carefully planned as the services in mainline churches down the street, was not so different, after all. Add a printed order of worship, complete with some prayers and responses, and the Pentecostal service would have been strikingly similar to the others. Certainly, there remained no remnants of the disruptive practices which had led to the excommunication of the members of this sect from their parent church.

The earlier zeal for tongues has been replaced by a zeal to erect Pentecostal denominations. The new churches enshrined the experience of tongues, but placed active emphasis on the forms and trappings of denominationalism. By the 1950's, the spiritual emphasis which had given the Pentecostals their thrust had declined and given way to denominational methodologies. Whereas earlier generations of Pentecostal leaders had emphasized spiritual experiences, their successors pushed for statistical growth, expanded physical facilities, and increased financial capabilities.

It is my feeling that had it not been for the spread of tongues within the major Protestant denominations, tongues would now be a dogma of a conservative (and numerically insignificant) group of sects. Speaking in tongues continues to be significant because it has become a part of the "charismatic movement," which cuts across the Catholic-Protestant line as well as denominational lines.

Two men and one organization, working concurrently, have been instrumental in bringing cross-fertilization between Pentecostals and the major Protestant denominations. The men are Oral Roberts and David du Plessis, and the organization is the Full Gospel Businessmen's Fellowship International.

Roberts' rise from the pastorate of a small church to become one of the world's best known religious leaders is a success story all its own. But what Oral Roberts achieved, above anything else, was to put the beliefs of Pentecostals before a national audience — they became credible to a large audience who otherwise would never have heard of them. Roberts' Pentecostal views became a commonplace to the millions who began to follow and support him. His resources and effectiveness far outstripped all of the other Pentecostals put together. His success and unorthodox methods piqued his own denomination's leaders. When, in the 50's, he tried to give them funds for a suitable office building in Memphis, Tennessee, they rejected the idea. Their world headquarters remain in a little town of less than one thousand, Franklin Springs, Georgia.

The key to Roberts' success was his ability to develop support among non-Pentecostals. The relatively small number of Pentecostals and their limited resources would never have permitted the ambitious multimillion-dollar programs he envisioned. The year that he changed to the Methodist Church, the income for the various Roberts enterprises — with a staff of 600, six foreign offices, ORU, TV, radio, publishing, etc. — was $6.4

million. The following year, receipts exceeded $13 million, and within three years, well over $20 million. In 1972, the biggest year ever, income approached $25 million.

Until about 1960, Roberts never wavered in acknowledging his denominational affiliation as a Pentecostal. Had he, like Aimee Semple McPherson, been interested in establishing a separate denomination, he had all the components available for such a move. He never indicated any interest in that. Instead, he de-emphasized denomination and stressed religious experience. In 1961-62, when Roberts began stressing speaking in tongues, thousands of his supporters in the mainline denominations also began testifying to this experience.

Roberts' philosophy dovetailed with the efforts of another Pentecostal preacher, David du Plessis. Whereas Roberts was the Pentecostal champion who slew the Goliaths, du Plessis worked quietly behind the scenes. Where Roberts worked with the masses, du Plessis sought to influence the decision-makers.

In 1950, David du Plessis accepted the challenge of working through established ecumenical circles to bring about a better understanding of speaking in tongues and the Pentecostal movement.[23] His efforts, especially with the World Council of Churches, began to pay off. Official attitudes softened, tolerance and interest increased. Du Plessis's efforts were instrumental in developing among major Protestant bodies a stance which permitted the new tongues speakers to stay in their denomination.

The Full Gospel Businessmen's Fellowship International (FGBMFI) was founded by Roberts supporters in 1951. Its single purpose was to spread tongues speaking among major Protestant denominations. Its first and only president is Demos Shakarian, a California dairyman and an original trustee of the Oral Roberts Evangelistic Association.

The FGBMFI practiced the success formulas of Roberts, who spoke at their annual banquets (until he joined the Methodist Church, that is). Soon the organization was making moderate inroads into the major churches.

The intent of FGBMFI was not to become another tongues-speaking denomination, nor to channel new converts into Pentecostal churches. Rather, it sought to gain new tongues speakers who would remain in their own denominations and therein witness to the vitality of their newly found experience.

The first widespread public recognition of the effectiveness of FGBMFI, Roberts, du Plessis, and others came from an article published by *Time Magazine* in 1960. The event which was treated in the article has been emphasized out of proportion; yet, the fact that media coverage snowballed is of itself significant.

The article was a report on a controversy over tongues in a wealthy Episcopal church in Van Nuys, California. The rector, Dennis Bennett, defended from the pulpit his personal belief in tongues. As historian G. Hugh Wamble has reported it, Bennett was introduced to glossolalia by some Episcopal laymen. "He studied the phenomenon and soon experienced it. He concluded that glossolalia is a rational experience, devoid of hysteria, in which one expresses love and devotion to God."[24]

Prior to the outbreak of glossolalia in his church (some seventy families shared his perspective), Bennett had enjoyed a spectacular success as a pastor in terms of growth, finances, and personal and professional respect. He could not be dismissed as a freak. A businessman who later decided to enter the ministry, he had graduated from Chicago Theological Seminary and entered the Congregational ministry. Later, he turned to the Episcopal Church.

Bennett's public accounting coalesced with a mushrooming growth of tongues in non-tongues-speaking churches. Within three years, every major Protestant denomination had outbreaks of tongues, as did several prominent universities.[25] With the rise of these new tongues speakers, attention of those interested in this phenomenon shifted from the Pentecostals to their new converts, the charismatics.

Pentecostal groups objected to du Plessis's ecumenical activities and broke fellowship with him. Meanwhile, many Pentecostal leaders had also cooled on Roberts. Long before Roberts had made any moves towards Methodism, the largest of the Pentecostal groups, the Assemblies of God, refused to let any of their ministers work for him. Those who did so in defiance of this edict lost their ministerial orders and denominational affiliation. Then, at the 1961 Pentecostal World Conference, assembled in Jerusalem during Pentecost, conservatives pushed through a policy of "no compromise" with other denominations.[26]

But more critical, from the Pentecostalist view, was the theological diversity of these new adherents. Many of the charismatics rejected the rather unsophisticated theological formularizations of their generally less educated brethren. Moreover, most of them totally ignored the lingering holiness social codes. To the horror of the

Pentecostals, some charismatics even continued to drink alcoholic beverages and to smoke — clear symbols of the "world" and flagrant examples of "carnal conduct."

This disenchantment was aptly stated by Ray H. Hughes, president of Lee College, which is supported by the Church of God (Cleveland, Tennessee). He asserted that the new breed put an . . . "overemphasis on faith alone as the adequate qualification for receiving the Spirit, ignoring holiness and tolerating carnal conduct, using noisy syllables as pump-primers or aids to tongues, using breathing techniques as aids to the Spirit's in-breathing, profaning glossolalia by using it in public demonstrations and scientific experiments, claiming a power to impart spiritual gifts (a power belonging only to the Spirit) and accepting the false explanation that glossolalia is a phenomenon to be understood psychologically, not spiritually."[27]

Pentecostals, the very group which once had been subjected to ridicule for believing in tongues, now strangled their own child. Their rigidity precluded any understandings of tongues other than their own. This kind of separatist stance had at one time enabled them to survive. They were ridiculed, ostracized, and not taken seriously — yet, all the while, they continued to grow. They regarded it a privilege to preach and to witness to the unique truth to which they considered themselves privy. But something happened along the way. Their tongues experience became synonymous with their denomination. The zeal with which they had spread their beliefs was now diluted with a drive to build denominations.

This change in direction came at a critical juncture — at the very time when many in major Protestant denominations were ready to look seriously at their own distinctive forms of witness. While the Pentecostals had an excellent opportunity for reorientation, owing to their comparatively short existence, their fascination with themselves precluded their accepting the challenge. Pentecostals had for 70 years witnessed to the power of the tongues experience within a context of rigorous discipline. They were shocked over the unwillingness of new tongues recipients in mainline churches to accommodate their expressions of tongues to Pentecostal principles.

The failure of Pentecostalism to rise to the challenge created a primordial crisis comparable in some degree to the crisis of Methodism after the holiness controversy. Methodism's distinctive witness, Christian perfection, was lost because it had been poorly interpreted and no one was capable of reappropriating it for that time in history. Now Pentecostals, whose sole ecclesiological reason for being is their witness to the importance of glossolalia, have denied themselves the harvest of their 70 years' labor. And in so doing, they have reinforced the inclinations of new charismatics to stay in their own denominations. That development has posited the issue as it has never been posited before. The issue is: Can you authentically believe in and practice glossolalia and remain in major Protestant denominations?

When social standards are no longer so exclusivistic as to permit differentiation between Pentecostals and others . . . when the order and decorum of Pentecostal services are slowly approaching that of other groups — when these and other accommodations have been made, then what is the real basis for the continuing existence of Pentecostal churches?

Admittedly, that is a rhetorical question, for Pentecostal denominations do preach more than tongues. But because of their failure to aid, encourage, and bring resources to the fledgling tongues speakers within Pentecostalism, the momentum for the effective spreading of tongues has shifted to the charismatics. Increasingly, the charismatics will be in the forefront of the tongues movement. With no denominational axe to grind and with a more flexible self-understanding, they will have the potential for significantly affecting the church of tomorrow. For that reason, it's easy to predict that speaking in tongues is here to stay.

APPENDIX: A REVIEW IN UNDERSTANDING

As I stated in the preface, before one can say, "I agree" or "I disagree," he must first be able to say, "I understand." The one uncontroversial thing that can be stated about tongues and the people who speak in tongues is that there is more misunderstanding than understanding.

The following quiz is not dependent upon the preceding material, nor is it entirely separate. In the initial preparation of *I Once Spoke in Tongues*, these were questions which I asked myself before proceeding to write. The answers were written when I concluded my research. I suggest that you take this quiz as a review of the material which you have read. You'll also gain some additional information.

Answer "True" or "False":

T. F.

1. The person who speaks in tongues has no control over when this activity occurs.   ___ ___
2. Those who speak in tongues do so regularly, especially in church worship services.   ___ ___
3. People who speak in tongues have serious emotional problems; they have difficulty with depression, especially.   ___ ___
4. Speaking in tongues is really another language or dialect.   ___ ___
5. Speaking in tongues is such a deeply religious, and emotional experience that it should not be examined closely.   ___ ___

T.   F.

6. Tongues speakers are mostly lower
class, illiterate persons.

7. To believe that speaking in tongues is
a valid experience also requires a belief
in the literal, verbal inspiration of the
Bible.

8. Tongues can be learned much as
foreign languages are.

9. What is known today as speaking in
tongues is not the same as the experience which is described in the Bible.

10. Speaking in tongues is a badge of
identification which authentically separates the speaker from other Christians.

11. The Bible does not support speaking
in tongues.

12. The Bible assigns great importance to
speaking in tongues.

13. Speaking in tongues is *the* evidence of
a person's having received the baptism
of the Holy Spirit.

14. Speaking in tongues died out during
the first century of the church and
was not revived until the twentieth
century with the emergence of the
Pentecostal churches.

15. The Pentecostal denominations have
been most receptive to the tongues-
speaking movements in mainline denominations.

The answers? With some qualifications, *all* of the above statements are false. Please read on.

1. *The person who speaks in tongues has no control over when this activity occurs.*

False. There are some who seek this experience and believe that God moves the tongue, gives the sounds, and determines the time to speak. They believe that if the seeker will give himself completely in the search for this experience, God will eventually reward his diligence and sacrifice, and cause him to speak in tongues.

This belief, however, has been disproved by the practice of many in the charismatic ranks. They speak in tongues at will. I know a minister who claims to speak in tongues while he is driving his car or shaving. He and others do not wait for a special time or place. They, and not God, initiate the speaking. They force the air from their lungs through their voice box. Though some tongues recipients may exhibit compulsive behavior, their habits do not arise out of their tongues speaking; their emotional patterns would be present whether or not they spoke in tongues.

2. *Those who speak in tongues do so regularly, especially in church worship services.*

False. Many who have this experience, especially in Pentecostal denominations, speak in tongues very rarely — as infrequently as three or four times a year, and then at times of extreme emotional highs or lows. A Pentecostal church service may go by without anyone audibly speaking in tongues.

This pattern is changing as persons in major Protestant denominations begin to experience this phenomenon.

Increasingly, they attach importance to speaking in tongues regularly and frequently. This may be in their private devotions or in prayer groups and retreats, but seldom is it in church services.

3. *People who speak in tongues have serious emotional problems; they have difficulty with depression, especially.*

False. It was long assumed that people who spoke in tongues were emotionally handicapped. Indulgence in tongues speaking was considered an external expression of an internal disturbance. Interestingly, a recent study by the National Mental Health Institute found that quite the contrary is true. In the groups studied, the researchers found that people who spoke in tongues maintained a better state of emotional well being than did non-tongues speakers.

4. *Speaking in tongues is really another language or dialect.*

False. Although, it is held by some to be true. Some persons who speak in tongues identify their utterances as being in a national language or local dialect. For example, in his book, *Yes, Lord*, Harold Bredesen relates an experience in which he witnessed to an Egyptian woman. Bredesen prayed in tongues and the woman expressed amazement because she recognized Bredesen's expressions as being Archaic Egyptian.

Also, in a recent magazine article, actor Pat Boone told of his family's tongues experiences, and once his expressions were identified as a native language.

It is certainly true that tongues speaking has the rhythm of an articulated language. Also, a particular tongues statement may seem to relate to a particular family of languages. However, few investigations find tongues to be a "language" in any commonly understood definition of the word.

Because considerable personal testimony connecting tongues to specific languages is finding its way into print, there will no doubt be increased efforts to prove or disprove the relationship. Until more evidence is produced, I will continue to believe that tongues speaking is distinct from national languages or local dialects.

5. *Speaking in tongues is such a deeply religious and emotional experience that it should not be examined closely.*

False. In any area of religious concern, sensitivity to the feelings of others is an important attribute; however, a Christian also has the obligation to achieve self-understanding. The Christian's life is one of trying to understand himself and his relationship to God and his neighbors. This need for understanding embraces all religious experience, including tongues. Intentional ignorance, whether it hides under a disguise of piety and pride or is guarded by fear and false religiousness, only stunts the development of personhood and the process of self-understanding.

6. *Tongues speakers are mostly lower-class, illiterate persons.*

False. This kind of evaluation is relative — that is, poor or illiterate *in relation to whom.* It is true that in the early days of the tongues-speaking denominations, their membership came from the lowest socioeconomic sector. But there has been an evolution which has moved tongues speakers up the socioeconomic scale. The cross-fertilization with Episcopalians, Presbyterians, Methodists, etc., is contributing to this escalation.

An interesting example of this escalation is an incident involving Alabama's Governor George Wallace, a leading Methodist layman. A victim of an attempted assassination during the 1972 presidential campaign, Wallace had his wife place a call requesting Oral Roberts to pray for his paralyzed limbs. Roberts began praying for the governor over the phone. While Roberts was praying, Mrs. Wallace, who was listening on an extension, began speaking in tongues for the first time in her life.

7. *To believe that speaking in tongues is a valid experience also requires a belief in the literal, verbal inspiration of the Bible.*

False. While the great majority of people who speak in tongues are fundamentalists in belief and literalists in scriptural interpretation, there is a growing number (though a small number, still) of tongues speakers who are not. This is especially true of charismatics from the major denominations. Also, an increasing psychological interest in tongues portends nonliteral biblical perspectives.

8. *Tongues can be learned much as foreign languages are.*

False. Some evidence suggests that tongues speaking is a learned experience: People who receive tongues have heard others. Many times there is mimicry of key words and phrases. In fact, psychologist Dr. John P. Kildahl,

138

following extensive investigation, concluded that tongues *is* a learned phenomenon.[28]

Yet, the acquisition of tongues remains a different process than the learning of a language. Tongues speaking involves a unique kind of receptivity and preparation which is not readily explained. In my own experience, there was a time when I could not speak in tongues despite my very best desires and efforts. Then, boom! one morning I could. This breakthrough was followed by a period of faltering attempts. Finally, there was fluency.

Now, despite my having rejected the importance of tongues in my own life, I can still speak in tongues at will. Evidently, after one has spoken in tongues, he never loses the facility.

Perhaps a full answer to the question of whether tongues can be learned will have to wait until someone who has spoken in tongues attempts to teach tongues in the manner that he would teach a second language — specifically, without the religious overtones.

9. *What is known today as speaking in tongues is not the same as the experience which is described in the Bible.*

False. Proving either position is difficult. One might object that the same logic used to answer "false" can also be used to answer "true." There are no tape recordings with which to prove or disprove this proposition. There are some rather good descriptions in the New Testament which suggest a similarity between tongues speaking then and today. First Corinthians relates problems with tongues in the church in Corinth which are similar to some of the problems encountered in modern churches where speaking in tongues takes place.

10. *Speaking in tongues is a badge of identification which authentically separates the speaker from other Christians.*

False. Unfortunately, a great many people do "wear" tongues as an I.D. badge. This stance cannot be supported biblically, however.

There are tongues-speaking persons who place so much importance on this act that they exclude all other religious experiences. They form special cells within their churches; they exhort their friends who have not yet received tongues to open themselves to this gift. In fact, there are incorporated nonprofit organizations whose sole goal is to initiate other persons into tongues. The end result is that tongues speakers imply, either implicitly or explicitly, that their experience of tongues has added a unique and pervasive quality to their Christian experience — so much so that they are better Christians and better persons than before.

Worn as a badge of identification, tongues results in walls of division, mistrust, and resentment. Much of the strong negative feeling that many church people hold against tongues speaking can be traced to this misuse.

11. *The Bible does not support speaking in tongues.*

False. In no place does the Bible admonish against speaking in tongues. Although the Apostle Paul places certain restrictions upon the use of tongues, in I Corinthians 14:39 he specifically states, ". . . forbid not to speak in tongues." Indeed, in the same chapter where he lays down rules governing the use of tongues in

140

religious services, he claims to speak in tongues more
than anyone in the church at Corinth. (I Cor. 14:18)
Though tongues speaking was not in any sense a pre-
requisite for acceptance as a Christian in the early
church, it was an experience which was shared by many.

12. *The Bible assigns great importance to speaking
in tongues.*

False. There are sixty-six books in the Bible, and only
three of them mention tongues. There are 1,189 chapters
in the Bible, and only seven refer to tongues. There are
31,162 verses, and only twenty-two mention tongues.
Sheer quantity is not, of course, a proper criterion for
evaluating scriptural teachings. By the same token, however, a practice which is mentioned so seldom hardly
deserves the attention that some give tongues, and the
benefits do not seem to be commensurate with the
cleavages that are created.

13. *Speaking in tongues is the evidence of a person's
having received the baptism of the Holy Spirit.*

False. John the Baptist said, "I have baptized you
with water: but he (Jesus) will baptize with the Holy
Spirit." This statement is quoted, with attribution to
John, in all four Gospels and twice in Acts. In none of
these places is there a reference to tongues. In Acts 11,
Peter describes to the Council in Jerusalem the outpouring of the Spirit which took place in the house of
Cornelius in Corinth — where they spoke in tongues —
but in making that report he doesn't mention tongues.

Clearly, the Acts of the Apostles describes the several
outpourings of the Holy Spirit as being the fulfillment
of the statement which was made by John the Baptist.

But instead of the author's using the word "baptism" to describe the outpourings, he uses phrases such as "they were filled with the Holy Spirit." In another place, the wording is "received the Holy Spirit." But in only three of the seven places does tongues accompany the infilling or reception.

Within the context of the world-view of the early church, tongues was a miraculous sign which accompanied and validated the coming of the Holy Spirit. Just as the birth of Jesus was reported in the Gospels as having been accompanied by the miraculous, so also is the age of the Holy Spirit ushered in by the miraculous.

The New Testament clearly teaches that all Christians have the Holy Spirit, and the overriding evidence of this presence is never tongues. It is, rather, such qualities as love, joy, peace, patience, kindness, goodness, faithfulness, gentleness, and self-control.

14. *Speaking in tongues died out during the first century of the church and was not revived until the twentieth century with the emergence of the Pentecostal churches.*

False. Throughout church history there have been outbursts of speaking in tongues. In the recent past, groups which have experienced outbreaks include the Mormons and the Catholic Apostolic Church (Irvingism); the Shakers, in the 18th Century, and one branch of the Huguenots in France, during the 17th Century.[29] In none of these instances, however, did tongues gain the circulation that it did in the twentieth century. In this century, instead of splintering into nothingness as the earlier outbreaks did, tongues spread and grew into a strong and world-wide sectarian force.

15. *The Pentecostal denominations have been quite receptive to tongues-speaking movements in mainline denominations.*

False. Initially, the Pentecostals responded positively to the rise of tongues in mainline denominations — they saw the outbreaks as a validation of their own struggle and as a fruition of their many years of effort. But this response did not last.

Two things changed the Pentecostals' response.

First, the new tongues speakers failed to leave their denominations and join the Pentecostals, a rebuff which most Pentecostals found hard to accept. This is better understood when one recalls that the Pentecostal denominations were formed because their people had been ousted from the mainline churches. Since these ousters were, in essence, the reason for the establishment of Pentecostal churches, continued membership in the mainline churches by tongues-speaking persons seemed inappropriate to the Pentecostals. In essence, it called into question their reason for existence.

Second, among Pentecostals there remain vestiges of the prohibitions against alcoholic beverages, card playing, smoking, dancing, motion pictures, etc. Some of the adherents to tongues do not honor these restrictions, and for some Pentecostal leaders it is reprehensible even to consider having fellowship with a tongues-speaking person who smokes and/or imbibes.

ACKNOWLEDGMENTS

1 Song — "I'm Going Through" (Dayton, Tennessee: R. E. Winsett, 1929).

2 James F. White, *New Forms of Worship* (Nashville: Abingdon Press, 1971), p. 106. Used by permission.

3 White, pp. 21f.

4 White, p. 48.

5 Luther B. Dyer, ed., *Tongues* (Jefferson City, Missouri: LeRoi Publishers, 1971), p. 47.

6 John P. Kildahl, *The Psychology of Speaking in Tongues* (New York: Harper & Row, 1972), pp. 73f. Used by permission.

7 Kildahl, p. 80.

8 Kildahl, pp. 83f.

9 Kildahl, p. 41.

10 Catholic Biblical Association of Great Britain, *The Holy Bible* (Camden, New Jersey: Thomas Nelson & Sons, 1966), p. 237.

11 Article by W. G. Putman in *The New Bible Dictionary*, J. D. Douglas, ed. (Grand Rapids, Michigan: Eerdmans, 1971), p. 1286.

12 Mrs. M. Beeching, article in *The New Bible Dictionary*, J. D. Douglas, ed. (Grand Rapids, Michigan: Eerdmans, 1971), p. 1038.

13 Reinhold Niebuhr, *Leaves from the Notebook of a Tamed Cynic* (New York: World Publishing, 1929), pp. 122f. Used by permission.

14 David Wilkerson, *The Cross and the Switchblade* (New York: Random House, 1963).

15   Wayne A. Robinson, ed., *What's a Nice Church Like You Doing in a Place Like This* (Waco, Texas: Word Books, 1972), p. 15.

16   Ernst Troeltsch, *The Social Teachings of the Christian Churches* (London: 1931).

17   Albert C. Outler, ed., *John Wesley* (New York: Oxford University Press, 1964), p. 19.

18   Vinson Synan, *The Holiness-Pentecostal Movement in the United States* (Grand Rapids, Michigan: Eerdmans, 1971), p. 37.

19   Synan, p. 53.

20   Synan, p. 51.

21   Synan, p. 54.

22   John MacQuarrie, *Twentieth-Century Religious Thought* (New York: Harper & Row, 1963), p. 125.

23   Dyer, p. 45.

24   Dyer, p. 49.

25   Dyer, p. 49.

26   Dyer, p. 51.

27   Dyer, p. 51.

28   Kildahl, p. 74.

29   Dyer, pp. 24-40.